Beginnings, Middles, & Ends

Sideways Stories on the Art & Soul of Social Work

By Ogden W. Rogers

White Hat **Communications**

Beginnings, Middles, & Ends
Sideways Stories on the
Art & Soul of Social Work

by Ogden W. Rogers

Published by:

 White Hat **Communications**

Post Office Box 5390
Harrisburg, PA 17110-0390 U.S.A.
717-238-3787 (voice)
717-238-2090 (fax)
http://www.socialworker.com

Note: The names and identities of individuals mentioned in this book have been carefully disguised in accordance with professional standards of confidentiality.

Cover Photo Credit: Image from BigStockPhoto.com © Nguyen Thai

Library of Congress Cataloging-in-Publication Data
Rogers, Ogden Willis, 1955-
  Beginnings, middles, & ends : sideways stories on the art & soul of social work / by Ogden W. Rogers.
    pages cm
  Includes bibliographical references.
  ISBN 978-1-929109-35-7
  1. Social workers. 2. Social case work. 3. Social service--Practice. 4. Rogers, Ogden Willis, 1955- I. Title. II. Title: Beginnings, middles, and ends.
  HV40.35.R644 2013
  361.3--dc23

                    2013019570

Contents

2. Middles

3. The Dialogs of Hanna

4. Ends

Acknowledgments

I appreciate so many folks who gave me the support to write this book. My wife Carol, and my sons Brendan and Colin, are the foundation of my life. My parents; my first supervisor, Louise Meister; and Arthur Schwartz, dear colleagues, are no longer alive in this world, but are the spirits of my efforts. My "old" mentors, Tom Vassil and Paul Ephross, my students, and colleagues are the engine of this wonderful pursuit called social work for which this book is written.

Thank you to Jennifer Clements, Stephen M. Marson, and Kryss Shane for their valuable feedback on an earlier version of the manuscript for this book, and to Gary Grobman for his editing expertise.

Thanks to my editor and colleague Linda Grobman and White Hat Communications for taking the risk of such an off-beat effort as this.

And then, of course, there's Hanna.

Preface (No seriously, please read this)

Welcome to this book. I'm glad you took the time to come this far to read it. This book is an irregular collection of bits and pieces that are part of the crazy-quilt of my social work life. Many of the moments of this book have grown from experiences I've had or stories I used in my lectures with students or told in my office with clients. Some of them have grown from essays I wrote for others, for personal or professional reasons.

It's my hope that some of the things here might make some moment in your thinking or feeling grow as a social worker. If they provoke a smile, or a tear, or a critical question, it's worth it. Some of the pieces are experiences from my interior and may not seem immediately relevant to your life as a social worker. If you get bored, skip a piece, and read something else.

I will tell you right up front that I feel it is a pretty arrogant thing to write a book like this. Personal narratives can seem a little self-centered, and I apologize right "from the get-go" if you get a little sick of my shared thoughts, feelings, and observations. I wrote this book for colleagues, social work students and their teachers, and to be very honest, for myself. In the seasons of studying social work, students have to read a lot of textbooks and professional literature. I know, I've had to read a lot of those things, and they are good to read...but sometimes, it's good to take a break and just read something that's just a little off center and not in APA style! Something to read, well, just for the heck of reading.

The idea for this book came from what I call a "sideways story." A sideways story is some little (or big!) moment in life when you thought you were doing one thing, but you ended up learning another. A sideways story can also be a poem, or prose, that, because of the way it is written, may not be all that direct in its meaning. What's nice about both clouds, and art, is that you can look at them and just resonate. I think that can be good for both the heart and the mind.

Some months ago, I received a letter from a professor with whom I had studied in undergraduate school. He had been the chaplain at the college I attended, and I remembered him as a gentle man of integrity. He had seen an article about some work I was doing in the college alumni magazine, and sent me a letter commending my efforts. I was quite flattered.

In the letter, he wrote that he was reminded of a story I had written as a young man, apparently for one of his classes. The story, he said, was about an old man whom I had come to know while working in a hospital, and who had died. A line in the story he remembered went: "Mr. Etters died yesterday. And with his death, a story ended. Not just a person had died, but a history, memories, and an unfolding story of life that could only be told by this one man also ended." He told me that he had never forgotten that story, and that he reflected upon it as he had gone into semi-retirement and pastoral counseling of persons with terminal illnesses. I was deeply moved that anything I had ever written had "stuck" with somebody.

While the story sounded familiar, I did not remember it, and I went scouring about in my files, looking at all my undergraduate work, to see if I had kept it. (I am a world class "pack-rat" and have thrown away almost nothing in my life!) Looking off and on for weeks, I could not find the story anywhere in my files. In the search, however, I had come across all sorts of odds-n-ends of things I had written.

I have always, since a small boy, been prone to writing some of my thoughts and observations down in various forms...almost all of it mostly for myself, or shared with small audiences of clients, students, or colleagues. Not really published.

It dawned upon me that like Mr. Etters (and everybody else in the world), I too had accumulated a basket of stories. In re-reading the scraps of essays, poems, and stories I had written, I considered that in some ways they were less about "me" (whatever that is!), and more about a life following a path of a social worker. I became arrogant enough to think you might enjoy reading some of them. I'm the hero in some of the stories; sometimes I'm the fool. I have probably learned more from the ones where I am the fool.

We talk nowadays about "research informed practice and practice informed research." Throughout my career, I've considered many theories. Theory about human behavior, theory about social change, theory about the nature of reality have all swirled about in my life and practice. I have used, and been used by, theories. At times throughout this book, you might find a footnote or two that might point you to investigate something further. But mostly, this book is about how a life in social work is made up of stories.

The stories in this book are sideways...not always linear. Each one of them had some meaning for me when I wrote it, but sometimes never what I intended. Taken together, they might reflect upon some of the things I have learned on the path to becoming a social worker. Perhaps, some of the writing might create some reflections for you, too. I might suggest that you consider each story after you've finished reading it. What (if anything!) might it have to do with living a social worker's life? (If nothing else, if you read them before bedtime they might induce sleep!)

A note on context:

In my occupational life, I have had a variety of experiences. I worked as an emergency medical orderly as an undergraduate, and as a psychiatric technician in a large private psychiatric hospital during my graduate school years. I worked as a clinical social worker in inpatient and outpatient community mental health and substance abuse, private and public medical and adult psychiatry and emergency and critical care medicine and long-term care in various agencies, and in disaster relief with the U.S. Public Health Service. I have done micro, mezzo, and macro work. I have served on task forces for domestic violence and served on several boards of private and governmental social service agencies. For a while, I worked in a state that had a license for "Psychiatrist's Assistant," which allowed me to practice like a psychiatric physician's assistant. The last decades have been as social work educator and consultant for state and federal agencies. I've been a volunteer with the American Red Cross since I was 15 years old and have done a little bit of everything with that organization. I am a married Caucasian male and have played a hand at raising two sons. I have a dog who likes to curl up on my lap.

A note on truth:

Obviously, none of the names in this book are the real names of people I know. Well, at least the names of clients, students, or persons who might have been in my direct authority or care. The "names have been changed to protect the innocent"...or even the guilty for that matter. The occasional friend, mentor, or public figure might be real.

The stories themselves have also been fictionalized, even though they are all true. Sometimes I've collapsed some events. Sometimes I've expanded some things. Sometimes I've mixed up some people and places and times. But, in some way, it all happened. I swear it.

Ogden W. Rogers
River Falls, Wisconsin, USA

1
Beginnings

The beginnings of things are powerful and mysterious in many ways. Social workers know it is important to "meet the client well"—that the beginning of a social work relationship, whether it's with an individual, a group, a family, or a community must be filled with clear engagement. The boundaries of a working relationship require orientation, communicated by a warm, welcoming, and assuring human presence. It is a time to develop the energy that can explore the problem at hand, and the solutions in the possibilities. Good beginnings unleash the potential for "doing good" in the world.

Many of Shakespeare's dramas begin in an apparent middle, but a significant part of the story is learning of beginnings that occurred before the play began. So, too, many of us who choose a social work path should explore the genesis of our own stories, which have led us to this dedicated expression of joining with people to find that place where society and the individual reach out for one another. We should develop a respect for where we've come, and where others have come, to the beginning of a social work moment.

Everything probably begins before one knows that it is beginning. But you've got to start somewhere!

Introductions

On my way to my first day of social work school, I came upon a woman who had just gotten out of a parking lot. She was walking in the same direction as I was, and as we were just paces from each other, I decided to say hello. "Hi, I'm Ogden, I'm starting at the social work school today," I said, "and you?"

She looked at me and smiled. "Oh...I'm Iona. I'm also starting at the school today."

We walked about a block more and talked about how beginnings were so exciting, and how lucky it was that we got into the School of Social Work. I said good-bye at the door and headed to registration.

The Dean was sitting at the first registration table, next to a woman who asked me my name. After I answered, she started to look for some cards with my information on them. The Dean put out her hand and said, "Oh, I know you...you're one of our new part-time students in the new extended program." I nodded.

"There are a number of us who don't think any of you will make it through."

I stood with my hand extended back. Stunned. Then, the woman I'd met in the parking lot walked up and sat down next to the Dean. She reached up and shook my hand. "Oh, hello. I'm Iona Hiland, the new Assistant Dean. Welcome to the School of Social Work. We're glad you're here."

I shook her hand. I reached back at the Dean. I shook her hand. "Well, ma'am, I hope to rise to the task."

Content, Process, and Boundary

I pulled aside the curtain. The patient was lying on the gurney, bandaged in several places and on an IV.

"Hi. How can I help you?"

"I'm not sure how. I don't know that I need help from you."

"Ahh. OK. Let me start again. What brings you here today?"

She laughed. "Ahh, an ambulance?"

I stepped back and bowed my head. "No. You are absolutely right. I'm in a hurry and I've started this all wrong. Please allow me to begin again."

I knocked on the door. "Hello? Mrs. Hamline? I'm Mr. Rogers. I'm a social worker here in the Emergency Department. Dr. Macalester told me that he's spoken with you about being admitted to the surgical unit, and he told me that you have concerns about your children at home. I'm wondering if we could talk together. Is there anything I can do to assist you?"

She smiled back. "Hello, Mr. Rogers. I'm Arella Hamline. I'm also a social worker at City Department of Social Services. I am glad you're here. I've apparently been in a serious auto accident, and they're going to admit me to the hospital, and I might go to the operating room tonight. I was on my way home from work. My children are probably at home now from school, but I haven't been able to contact them. I need to call my neighbor to see if she can watch them until I can get ahold of my mother and father who might be able to look after them. I don't have my phone, and I'm afraid I don't know her number."

"Ms. Hamline, it would be my pleasure to help. Let me slip over to my office and get my directory and a phone. I'll be right back."

She laughed. "It's a pleasure doing business with you."

Ahh. Beginnings. So important.

The Welcome Lecture

Welcome.

I understand that you are interested in joining our club called "Social Work." If you could spare a moment, I'd like to share some thoughts with you. You see, there are some risks and benefits in becoming a social worker, and I think one should consider them carefully before moving on.

Personal Risks

First of all, I think you should know that you can get killed doing this thing called social work. We work with marginalized and oppressed people. The social worker is involved with the most dangerous animal on earth: The Human Being. They are mammals, you know, and like all mammals, can lash out violently if frightened and cornered.

Consider this: two hungry dogs are in a corner staring at each other over a bone. Where is the last place you want to put your ankle? Right...anywhere near that bone. Yet, day in and day out, social workers put their hands right into that space between the dogs. They are hungry and frightened and angry. You need to be prepared if one starts to bite. So you see, you can get dead if you aren't smart and thinking about the risks at play with cornered people. And that's just a thought about the people we're trying to help. There are other mammals at the top of the food chain that can be even more dangerous.

Social workers are change agents...and some people hate change. They see it as a threat to all they have accumulated, like money and power. Some of these people are so attached to money and power that they will do anything to keep anyone from taking any of it. Depending on where you practice your social work, you might make them feel threatened, and they can lash out at you.

God forbid this country swings any more to the extreme of left or right (well, there's not much chance of a leftward swing in the foreseeable future, the "rightees" seem to have the stage right now). History has demonstrated that one of the first groups that get rounded up in the middle of the night, put into trucks, and taken someplace remote and dumped into a shallow grave are the folks who are "the helpers," "the do-gooders."

I just want you to know. You could take a bullet one day doing this work. I don't want it to be a complete surprise. It's gonna be surprise enough, and I hope that it never happens, but you gotta know. If you zig when you oughtta zag, if you're in the wrong place at the wrong time, you could get killed...or seriously injured. There are safer jobs. We social workers probably don't get killed as much as cops or fire fighters, but we walk places where it can get ugly. You've gotta think a little bit about your relationship to your own personal safety, and if you can handle a job with personal risks.

Psychological risks

It's not easy to think like a social worker. There are perspectives one has to acquire that make the world forever more complicated.

The "bi-focal" vision thing has a lot of weight. Once you acquire it, it becomes very difficult ever to look at things the same way again. Social work is about facilitating the challenges and strengths of little systems—like people—with the challenges and strengths of big systems—like communities, governments, and countries. A man named Schwartz[1] once said that social work is that place "where the individual and society reach out for one another." Think about that. That's a big idea.

So, you're always thinking about at least two things at the same time. How to help both the little guy and society at the same time. One has to be able to think like a juggler, or a surfer, or any master of multiple dimensions in motion.

A man falls into a ditch and you help him out: you've helped a man out of a ditch. Another man falls into the ditch and you help him out: you've helped another man out of a ditch. Another man fall into a ditch and the social worker, reaching down to help the man, cries out to all those who will listen: "Hey, people! Folks keep falling into this ditch! Can we all get together to think about doing something about this? How about a bridge?! Or a tunnel?! Does this ditch need to be here? Could we lay a pipe in there and cover this thing up? Waddya all think?"

Masters of the weird

Goethe[2] once said, "To think is easy. To act is hard. But the hardest thing in the world is to act in accordance with your thinking." I agree with much of that except the "thinking easy" part. To think is hard. Social workers are called to act all the time, but the true social worker will have thought through some of the hard questions: How individual are we? How collective? Where does the private trouble become the public concern? When is a right wrong, and a wrong right? Where does tolerance begin and end? What does the citizen owe to the society? What does the society owe to the citizen? I could go on, but the issue is to pursue the path of social work to make a commitment to struggle with ideas that will have no easy answers. And to give up on trying to think them through is irresponsible.

The world, it seems to me, falls into two groups of people—those who think in black and white and those who can appreciate the gray. Good social workers tend to be "gray-thinkers." The people who think in black and white often get furious with those of us who can appreciate the gray. They seek a simple world where everything falls into simple categories and straightforward solutions. Up, down; right, wrong; good, evil; and so on. It infuriates them when sneaky little aspects of gray reality tease apart their world view, and they hate that they need to have gray-thinkers help them out.

Life doesn't happen with a lot of very clear, black and white boundaries. There are some, but mostly everything is a constant state of negotiation in motion. One has to appreciate the way that a beach is "there," but in some ways, "not-there," in motion with each wave that breaks upon it.

Forests. Families. Crimes. Heroes. Beaches. Villains. Even life and death. Depending on how closely you look at them, you'll find that there are aspects of fuzziness about their edges. Things are rarely black and white. So, one has to be inquisitive, open, and courageous about entering into a world where humans get messy.

A woman walks into your office and says she has a problem. She says she thinks her husband likes to f*** their cow. (Watch it! Don't raise your eyebrows at me!) Now, to do this right, you have to be able to explore this, and nonjudgmentally. How long has she suspected this man had a problem having sex with the cow? Does she suspect he has sex with other farm animals? What behaviors in either the cow or the husband have given rise to this suspicion? Does the cow have a name? What is it, that now, she is telling you about this problem with having sex with the cow? What does she think about this practice? And here's the clincher...to really be able to help this woman, you're going to have to go someplace in your mind that can have some appreciation of this cow-sex going on in this family! (Okay, if you don't know what sex is, go ask your mom.) You will find out later that this whole story was just a test. She wanted to see how judgmental you are about the husband, because she wants to tell you about this real problem she has about having sex with her husband and a loaded gun. The core of helping people is the ability to empathize with them first. Humans are capable of great wonders, and terrible tragedies...you have to be able to go to places of imagination that most people will never wander. Some of the places you will have to go to in your mind will bring you great peace and strength. Some of the places where you will go will keep you up at night and shake your very core.

We know that the minute you create a box, there is an inside and an outside of the box. The social worker will be very happy to explore the inside...but will by nature also explore the outside. What is out there? Another box? (Yes!) And another, and another, and another. When you start to think like a social worker, it will sometimes separate you from the way a lot of other people think. I want you to be prepared for this. It can get lonely, and frankly, heavy. You will never see the world the same way once you start to appreciate the gray.

This thinking may isolate you from others sometimes. Not everybody appreciates empathy. Years ago, when Americans were shocked when terrorists used airplanes as bombs in 2001, the first thing I thought was, "Wow, how angry do you have to be to fly a plane into a building?" Lots of people around me at the time were not interested in the thoughts or feelings of people that they wanted to see as "the enemy."

Economic risks

Yeah...how old are you now? 18? 19? "Twenty-something?" You need to know that a social work life is a middle class life style at best. Depending on where you work, it could be pretty lower middle class. Oh, there are a few social workers out there who make beaucoup dollars, but pretty darned few. Just about any major coming out of a business college is going to make scads more money. Trust me, it's true.

Now you tell me that you're young and idealistic, and it's not really about making money. Well that might be fine right now, but I need you to be thinking about the long haul. This is called having a "psycho-temporal perspective." You have to be just as idealistic twenty years from now. When one is twenty and writes poetry, one is twenty. When one is forty and still writing poetry, one is a poet.

I have a neighbor. He works for a trophy company as a "sales manager." This guy doesn't even sell trophies. He just supervises about seven other guys who roam the country selling trophies. He works from home! I swear it's true. Anyway. This guy pulls in at least two and a half times more in income than I make...and I'm a full professor, I'm no schmoe! Honest, he coordinates, motivates, cajoles, supports, and problem solves just seven other guys, and he's pulling six figures!

Now...it gets to this. My kids have been riding around the neighborhood on trikes and bikes that I bought at the Fleet-Farm. His kids have been riding in motorized Barbie cars and such since they were toddlers. My kids are gonna be lucky I've got a twenty-year-old Volvo for a spare car. His kids will be tooling around in new Hummers.

The thing is, when I get outside and cut my grass, I have to be able to say to myself that my grass is just as green as his. He's a nice guy. I like his kids. (The Barbie cars are a noisy nuisance, but that's another story.) I am not jealous of his life. I have to be content with the economic path I have carved out for myself and my family, and be proud of the honesty of my work...being a social worker.

Social Risks

Sometimes, the streets where we walk are baking in the summer sun, and the asphalt sticks to your shoes. Sometimes the stuff that you walk in will be tracked into where you live. The people who live with you will need to know they will pay prices living with you.

Many folks do not walk through this life alone. The people you live with will have to know that you are also in a relationship with Social Work. "She" is a demanding lover who asks much of you. Sometimes, because of the boundaries of your practice, you will need to keep secrets from the people you love. This can be tough for you, and for them.

You will walk in from a long day with many burdens on your shoulders, and you will not be able to reveal all that weighs upon them to your lover. It will have to be enough that they know that it is weight that you have carried in from the day and belongs to your world of social work. You will not be able to share the details, only at best, the generalities.

Sometimes you will be the only thing in the world keeping somebody else alive. Your ego is the lending thread that supports a fragile hope in some desperate human being. That weekly appointment on Thursday is the only connection they have. The only thing right now that keeps them hanging on. Sometimes they will "stalk" you. Not with an intent to do you harm, but with the insecure need to see that you are still a permanent object in their life. If they drive around your house at night, it might creep out the people you live with. I remember my young son saying to me, "Daddy, that woman in the red Honda is driving around the house again." "Oh that's just somebody who's watching out for daddy...she wants to make sure I'm home and okay."

The Benefits

If you do social work right, few people will know about it. To be a social worker is always about giving it away. Making others feel and be empowered. Yes, it will be you who enters into the life of the Little Woman's Chowder Society some Wednesday night. It will be you who asks the group what they think the problem is. It will be you who will explore with them solutions. It will be you who asks Mavis to speak up, and you who asks Mabel to wait a bit until Mavis is finished speaking her piece. It will be you who will re-invite Mabel back into the conversation. And then you will ask Shirley, always the quiet one, what she thinks. But it will be they who finally make the decisions, invent the objectives, and accomplish the tasks that will make them feel like the greatest thing since sliced bread.

When you drive home that night, you might roll down the window of your car and howl at the moon. It is the lonely wolf howl of the social worker celebrating success. No one will understand how you have influenced things, how you have done some "good" in the world.

When you do "it" right, Social Work is a feeling that is larger than your own life. Psychologists call this feeling "flow state."[3] You've probably experienced it, perhaps when you were raising your voice in song with a chorus, or making that consciously-unconscious excellent pass on the basketball court, or a golf swing, or preparing a "perfect" meal. "It" happens when you know what you know, and you do it (in the middle, with other people) without needing to know it... (yet, you "know it").

Perhaps the next day, you might run into someone else in the club, another social work colleague, and casually note what you did the previous evening, and how you were "in the zone." If they are wise and experienced, they will nod, and smile, and validate your efforts. "It's so cool when that happens," they might say. "It's Social Work."

Latent Consequences

I was quite young, and my dad and I had just come back on the train from New York. As we walked out of Penn Station in Baltimore, we spent some time looking out below Charles Street at all the long deep scars of construction of what was going to be a new interstate highway.[4] Like all small boys, I marveled at all the big trucks and bull-dozers.

My dad was an urban planner at the time. I asked him what they were building.

He looked out northward to the horizon, thought for a while, and sighed. "It's either a great idea, or a terrible mistake. Only time will tell."

Politeness Counts

As I approached adolescence, my father taught me that if ever I found myself walking on a sidewalk alongside a woman, I should speed up my pace so that I could get in front of the woman as quickly and as far as possible.

When I asked him why I should do this, he replied. "It's the polite thing to do. As a man, you represent a potential threat from behind a woman. You represent much less of a threat if you are well in front, pulling away, and the woman can see you."

When I told him I didn't think that it was fair that I could be perceived as a threat to anybody, he said, "Some things are stupid and unfair. You can't help that. It's important to be polite anyway."

PigPigMotherf***er

When I was an undergraduate student, I had a job working in the emergency department of a Catholic hospital a few blocks down the street from my college. In high school, I had taught first aid and had been a disaster volunteer for the American Red Cross. The director of nursing thought I could be of use working as an orderly-corpsman in the emergency department, and elsewhere, as the hospital needed me, if the "E.R. was slow." It was here that I met another one of "those social workers," Morris Rosen.

My job was a wonderful gift of a job. I was in desperate need of money to go to college. The hours were mostly evenings and weekends, and if I pulled night shifts, there was always time to study. I wore "Doctor Kildare whites"—a side button tunic, slacks, and white leather tennis shoes that would inevitably get blood spattered on some evenings. It made for a grand entrance at some party, already under way at my frat house, when I got off of work. I always had a good story to tell.

In undergraduate school, I struggled about what I would do after college. A war in Vietnam was winding down, and a culture of distrust in all sorts of social institutions was still flourishing (and rightly so!). I had seen enough of the hospital to know that medicine was "broken." Physicians were very much at the mercy of a fragmented system that was increasingly fragmenting even more. Lawyers were just way "too establishment for me." I wasn't military officer material. I really didn't know what I wanted to do, so for now, I just concentrated on my studies in public health during the day and my job at the hospital at night.

But learning the ropes of the E.R. came only with much effort. I first had to learn how to take orders from Mrs. Pluto. And she knew how to give them.

Marti Pluto, RN, ran the emergency department like she had run the emergency surgical unit on a naval hospital ship a generation earlier in Korea. There was a practice of E.R. docs who staffed the physician ranks, and could bark orders at nurses and orderlies over patients, but there was no doubt who was in charge about just about everything else in the E.R.: Mrs. Pluto.

When I first came on board, fresh from hospital training, Mrs. Pluto made it clear to me that procedures in the Emergency Department were not the same as "up on the floors." My first job, she indicated, was to receive the patients from the triage nurse, escort them into a bay, take off their shoes, then their clothes, give them a gown and a name bracelet, and then take their "TPR," temperature, pulse, and respiration, and record it on their chart, notifying the charge nurse of the "occupation of the bay."

When I questioned if I should take a patient's TPR first, as the vital signs were the most important, Mrs. Pluto let me understand her philosophy of emergency medicine:

"Mr. Rogers," she began, ramrod straight, fists on hips. "The purpose of the emergency department is to save lives. The way you save lives is to bring order from chaos. People are chaos. They have individual identities with quirks that are unique to each one of them, those quirks probably being at the root of why they are presenting here, the emergency department, in dire straits. Here, we are in control. When you take away a man's shoes, he cannot run. When you take away a man's clothes he begins to lose control over his identity. When you give him his name on a bracelet, you demonstrate that you, and not he, are now in control of his name. When you control a man's name, you control a man. Then, and only then, do you take his temperature, pulse, and respiration. Do I make myself clear?"

I almost snapped a salute. "Yes Ma'am, Mrs. Pluto."

I enjoyed my job, as it was always filled with something new and dramatic, and I was quick on the uptake. Some days I assisted the orthopedic bay casting broken bones. Some days I was the second set of hands in the E.R. minor surgery. I was often the compression on a chest in a cardiac arrest. On weekends, I might get called to assist the pathologist in doing a stat autopsy. I was handy with "tubes, tape, and tools." and often ran for some errand on any floor. I was one of the few people in the hospital who might escort a patient from the front door, the E.R., then to "a bed" on "the floors," then to the back door, out of the morgue and into an undertaker's hearse. I learned a lot about how hospitals work, and don't work.

One of my jobs in the E.R. was to sit in the "psych" room with people who were in restraint. I was to make sure they didn't get out of restraint, and try to get their TPR. I liked working the psych room, because I was kinda fascinated by people who were psychotic. They said and did the strangest things.

I always thought it was curious that people who were crazy were brought to the emergency room. I mean, think about it: most of the time these people were scared, impulsive. Sometimes they wanted to hurt themselves, or others. It seemed to me that these folks needed safe, comfortable, stable, soft environments surrounded by caring people. The E.R. was this sterile, strange, hard place, filled with people in strange clothes and filled with sharp objects.

One night, I was called to sit next to a violent, frustrated man. The patient was a middle-aged man locked down onto the litter in leather shackles and four-point restraint. He seemed frantic and furious. He strained against the shackles. His clothes were wet from sweat and the struggle he had with the cops that brought him in. There was stale beer on his breath. He had a mantra that he kept repeating. "Pig, pig, motherf***er. Pig, Pig, motherf***er. Pig, Pig, motherf***er...."

I watched the man for a while, seated at the foot of his litter. When I was pretty sure there was no possibility of his escape from the shackles, and had ascertained the limits of his motions could not provide him a way to harm himself (or me!), I rose and calmly approached him.

"Would you like a little drink of water?" I asked. The man grew more furious, raged and chaffed even harder at the restraints, and screamed louder: "Pig, pig, motherf***er. Pig, Pig, motherf***er. Pig, Pig, motherf***er...." I moved away. He screamed louder. I moved closer. Even louder. I asked about if he'd like some ice chips. Louder still. Nothing I did seemed to offer him any calm. Getting his TPR made him even more agitated. He just ranted: "Pig, pig, motherf***er. Pig, Pig, motherf***er. Pig, Pig, motherf***er...."

Anyway, I was supposed to sit next to these often struggling, disturbed people until someone came to assess them for hospitalization.

Sometimes it was a shrink from the third floor psych unit. Most often, it was Morris.

Morris Rosen was the "county delegate," the man from the local community mental health center who made the mental health commitments to either the state hospital or the psychiatric unit on the third floor.

Everything about Rosen was completely unlike the E.R. The E.R. was hard and green and bright light and stainless steel and the smell of isopropyl alcohol. Morris was bald, dumpy, and rumpled brown corduroy, with shocks of fuzzy brown and gray hair sprouting from his temples. He always had the stump of a burnt out cigar stuck in the corner of his mouth. He carried this old leather briefcase filled with official papers and books with millions of telephone numbers.

Mrs. Pluto hated him.

When Morris would come through the ambo doors, hunched over and often humming to himself, Mrs. Pluto would scream at him to get rid of his cigar. Undaunted, Morris would just keep plugging through the swinging electric doors, reaching over the nurses' station to grab the chart, heading to the holding room. He would raise his left arm and wave through the windows. "Nice to see you, Marti! Always a pleasure!"

He was always nice to me.

Morris took a stool across from the man in the litter. I made a motion to leave my perch next to the litter when Morris furrowed a brow and waved me to sit back down. He sat quietly, holding his chin in his hand, crouched on the stool like some strange brown owl.

The guy on the litter just kept repeating his mantra, copious rivulets of sweat pouring from his brow. "Pig, Pig, motherf***er...pig pig motherf***er...pig pig...."

After what seemed like a long time, Morris leaned in slowly toward the patient and in what seemed like the most careful and serious way, he tilted his head and asked the guy, "Pig, Pig, motherf***er. Pig, Pig, motherf***er. Are you sure it's not supposed to be Motherf***er, Motherf***er Pig?"

The guy stopped. He cocked his head and stared at Morris. Looking at him. Seriously studying him. He shook his head, "No. It's got to be the other way around. Pig, Pig, Motherf***er."

Morris leaned again. "OK. OK. I get it. It's got to be Pig, Pig, Motherf***er. Motherf***er, Motherf***er Pig just won't do. But I don't know what would happen if it stopped being Pig, Pig, Motherf***er. Can you help me understand?"

The guy studied Morris some more and smiled a little bit. Then he started to explain to Morris how certain words needed to be said in certain ways. People get hurt when words are misplaced. Bad things happen. He, the guy, had been hurt when he had mis-spoken words. It had something to do with energy.

Morris asked him how. The guy came back with a rich and convoluted answer. I couldn't follow all the detail in it, but Morris acknowledged it and asked more. The conversation seemed crazy to me, with both men talking about things that seemed not to make sense. But Morris would latch onto some word or theme in the man's messages, and continue to make calm comments, and seek continued inquiries. In minutes, the frantic perseverant monologue had become a calm and engaged, if not (to my ear) totally psychotic, dialogue. Minutes later, the guy was out of four-point restraint and walking with Morris, voluntarily, up to the psych unit.

I buttonholed Morris some time later, as he was walking out the Ambulance Bay doors. "Hey, Morris...er, Mr. Rosen...that was amazing what you did with that guy. How'd you learn how to talk to that crazy guy and make him calm down?"

He smiled. "Inside every crazy guy is a sane guy looking to get out. Or it might be the other way around. I keep forgetting," he laughed.

"No, come on... seriously," I insisted.

"Well, as long as this is serious," he looked at me hard. "I went to social work school. I started learning there."

"Social worker?" I asked.

"Yeah, social worker," he replied. "It's a social work thing."

2 a.m.

The old man had come in via ambulance from Sinking Spring. He was tall, and one could tell he had once been strong and sinewy, but now he was wan and wasting away. His mind, it seemed, had shallowed in senescence, or perhaps just delirium. His breathing was labored, and he seemed in deep discomfort. His skin was clammy. His lungs had the sound of congestive heart failure, or emphysema. He was not really responsive.

His vitals taken, Desflures had ordered me to stick a Foley catheter[5] into him. They had left me alone to this task, and had gone out to order labs. There was a stricture somewhere in his urethra, and I couldn't pass a number 14 despite several attempts. I went down to a 12 and still it was a struggle. The old man moaned as I jammed into his penis. He relaxed a moment, and the catheter slid into place, and bright streams of urine flowed copiously.

I looked up and saw he was unconscious. I grabbed for a pulse and found it gone. "Oh, sh*t! Somebody get in here," I yelled. "This guy just went South...Hey, somebody!?! I need some help in here!"

Desflures came running with Ursula—they did a "half-court press" with me on the chest. He "called it" after what seemed like only minutes. As I cleaned it all up and prepared the body for the morgue, I couldn't stop thinking all my trauma with the Foley had caused the old man to die. I told this to Desflures as I tagged the body. He told me I was probably right, but it was gonna happen anyway in the next couple of days, and at least I had done it quickly. I had done the old man a favor.

"I pushed him over the edge, but you ordered me to do it." I looked at Desflures. He looked back. "I guess that makes us both murderers... or saints, depending on how ya look at it..." he said. "At three a.m. in the morning, such distinctions are trivial. Book 'im, Dano."

I took the old man up to the morgue. The undertaker slipped me a silver dollar before the end of the shift.

My Father's Tales

At the time, my daddy worked for the Bureau of Urban Renewal. He called himself an "urban planner." Mr. Bates and his family were over for a cookout in the back yard. We all heard a terrific crash, and nearby on Liberty Heights, there had been an auto accident. Mr. Bates, leaping up and running, arrived at the cars even before the fire fighters at the local engine house. There was a very seriously injured woman in one car, and he ripped his shirt to make bandages for her bleeding wounds. He barked orders at the fire fighters and clearly was commanding the situation until ambulances could arrive. When he returned to the cookout, he was covered in blood, so he washed up in our back yard with our hose and some soap. He was, I think, the first hero I had ever seen who hadn't been in a comic book. When I asked my daddy about him, he said Mr. Bates had been a social worker in the Red Cross in the war. I asked my dad what a social worker was. He said, "Little white haired ladies in tennis shoes."

I was confused.

At the time, my dad worked in the mayor's Bureau of the Budget. He called himself a "budget analyst." I was impressed with going down to City Hall with its high dome and wide marble steps. I would sit waiting for my dad in various city council and Board of Estimates meetings. I remember one meeting where a man was arguing fiercely for something, and afterward I asked my dad who he was. "Oh, that was Dr. Fratemann. He's a social worker." I asked him what a social worker was. "He's a guy who would throw his grandmother under a bus."

I was confused.

At the time, my father worked for the Department of Health. He called himself an "administrator." I remember one spring he was working out the details of some project that had been funded by a federal grant. It was a summer lunch program for kids who were poor. The kids who could get free lunches in school needed to get lunches when school was out for the summer. The lunches couldn't be made by school cafeteria staff, so my father was arranging with catering companies to make the thousands of lunches each day. He was arguing with the director of the program, a Miss Salomon, about how could you tell that the kids were getting the right amount of peanut butter on the sandwiches...because the caterers could spread the stuff so thin.

When I asked him about the phone call, he told me Miss Salomon was a social worker. I asked my father what a social worker was. He barked, "People who think pie drops from the sky, and all God's creatures are good."

I was confused.

At the time, my old man was tending bar at a rural Irish pub. After a lifetime of working in governmental bureaucracies, he had been used up and worn out. He had returned to the basic skills of his college days, the science of mixing drinks and listening to people tell stories as they slowly got drunk. I had spent four years at college studying the liberal arts, working in an emergency room to pay my bills, and had graduated to land a job as a psychiatric technician in a fancy private hospital.

After considerable thinking, I had ruled out going to law or medical school. I had looked closely at both professions, and the times were just not right. I had learned that hospitals had become big unwieldy machines that killed patients despite the best efforts of physicians. I had seen law schools churn out politicians who created wars that had killed tens of thousands of the young men of my generation. I wanted a profession that could make a difference, that could be personal and political at the same time, that skated down the middle, that knew when to say just the right thing to a crazy man struggling in the street, and a crazy politician relaxing in his office.

I sat at the bar and ordered a draft from my old man. I told him I was going back to grad school. That I had come to a decision about my career and how I would spend my life, and was happy about it. He smiled at me and said, "That's good...what are you gonna study?"

I took a drink from the beer and set down the glass. "I'm gonna be a social worker," I said.

My old man was confused.

Proper Noun

"No," she corrected me, "I'm not a schizophrenic."

"I have schizophrenia. It affects my thoughts, my moods, my behaviors, but it is not me."

"It's a disease," she said, "not a definition."

A Leg Up

That evening I had been called from the path lab to take a specimen to the morgue. It was 10 o'clock, and the technician wanted to go home. Stuff from the lab was rarely more than a bottle, so I had just walked up from the E.R. with nothing more than the morgue key. I was surprised when the technician handed me a whole male leg.

Bagged and tagged, I slung it over my shoulder like a ham. The foot stuck out. Late at night, I figured I would pass unnoticed if I took the freight elevator.

Passing the third floor, the elevator stopped for passengers—an aide with a patient in a wheelchair coming from the X-ray department. I slunk to the back of the car. The man in the wheelchair looked at me, and the leg. I looked down and could see beneath the blanket he was an amputee.

I was aghast and looked at the man. "I'm sorry," I said.

The man smiled weakly and reached out and shook the foot. "Take good care of it," he looked at me. "I got a hundred thousand miles on that one."

The Advice of Captain Don

"Look. Listen to me. I know what this is like. It seems scary, but it can be wonderful. Look up at Mt. Penn...see that light flashing in the distance? It's on the tower and it will flash all night, in a steady and constant fashion. If you just stay with that light, everything will be okay and the dawn will come up in the morning."

He was right.

E.R. # 662343472

I didn't stop to picture her as a smiling child
with six-year-old brown curls
that could toss carefree so much a part of games
that six-year-olds do play.

or even see her in her own right, not just another
temperature, or blood pressure or X-ray here or there.
a minor fever to cool and send quietly to bed
without so much as a thought of missing school on Monday.

and as things changed so quickly, as plucky life
in absurd reason began (no seeming reason for just
another cold) to look out from those brown eyes and question
the stranglehold of death approaching like a falsehood?

i still did not see crayons or accoutrements of children.
time became so present, so present as it always does when
unseen in the green lit corridors i catch steps and
run, the ceiling, scientific angel speaks: "E.M.E., pediatrics,

E.M.E., pediatrics."
and crashing doors through darkness do not disturb the sleep
of many while efficient hearts pick up their paces to clean
pump minds and hands that suction, and inject, or guide dials

in scientific haste. i saw now the febrile convulsions, the
high white count, the offset gases of the blood. in the corner
the only one in Black tries touching the unseen, tries pushing
other buttons we have no time to think about.

somewhere outside the always dim of I.C.U. morning played
over the mountains, and bright Sunday reflected from the
buildings downtown. another shift was over, another
night had passed and still there were no thoughts of smiles

as a quivering little body began to trigger tubes and monitors.
the life lines of plastic and saline reached down and in

to those unseen places that would still grasp. to places that
might still remember trees and zoos and games.

but in the sunlight everything had changed. And walking down
eleventh street I looked for children to see if smiles still
lived and brown curls did not paste in sweat to foreheads. I
spat upon the science of the darkness which lights only

organism and makes us dwell so presently without smiles.
but that too, passes, and only a quick hope could follow me
down the street, geese flew over in the springtime
and one could only feel small against the world.

*Note: This poem was originally published in 1977 in The Agon, Reading,
PA: Albright College.*

Going With the Defense

Whatever a client brings to you, accept it as a gift. There are thoughts, feelings, and behavior, seen and unseen, and whatever emerges is something to be tracked, followed, and used to help the relationship.

Never stop a running man.

Run with him and wave others off who might stop him. Slowly slow your pace, travel to a place where the running no longer serves a purpose, and perhaps sitting and talking will emerge.

Some wise workers call this "exhausting the resistance" or "going with the defense."[6] I like to think of it as simply unwrapping a gift and using it.

Day-At-a-Glance (age 19)

Friday

0600. up, dressed, and down to the cafeteria. Scarf down some eggs, juice, and a donut and "slop" for an hour. Slop: take trays from fellow students through a window. Dump waste down a little hole. Put trash down another hole. Throw silverware into a plastic tub. Stack everything else in piles that the "feeder" can throw into the dishwasher machine. Do this until 0745.

0800. HIST. "Barbarians to 1642." Try desperately to stay awake as prof drones on about Pepin the Short and the Carolingians. I have no idea why I took this class.

0900. PHIL. "Individual and Society." Prof is the campus chaplain and today we are talking about his decision to volunteer into the army in WWII. Most of us in the room are clearly aware we have just dodged the Viet Nam draft bullet. There's a guy in the back who did a tour and got wounded in the Tet Offensive. Whenever he talks about it, he cries.

1000. campus center. Goof off in the corner with TEKEs. Coffee. 'nother donut. Absent mindedly read the front section of the *Philadelphia Inquirer* while Noodles drools over the freshman girl who's been hanging with us this past week. Listen to Kung espouse the genius of Nietzsche. Wonder if I'm supposed to work lunch today. I forget. Wander to back of cafeteria to check the schedule board. Sh*t. I have to work lunch.

1115. scarf down lunch of chicken noodle soup and grilled cheese. Slop dishes from 1130 to 1245.

1300. SOC "Sociology Of Poverty." Cool prof once walked in Selma with Dr. Martin Luther King. We spent much of the hour looking at the cost of a pound of hamburger as you go from supermarkets in the suburbs to the inner city on the same radial street. The closer to the center of the city, the higher the price of the beef.

1400. Back to dorm. Shower. Do about half-hour of Stats homework due Tuesday. Have no idea if I am solving the problem right.

Dress in the Dr. Kildare whites and start booking down 13th Street to the hospital. Pass kids coming out of the high school who make stupid comments.

1530. have clocked-in and reported to E.R. nurses' station. Report is under way. Nothing in the main bays. Hot appendix in observation Bay 1 is waiting for a bed on 3 north. I get a page to set up leg traction on 5 south. Toodle up to do the "erector-set" on a guy whose leg is all in plaster after falling off his motorcycle.

1600. Back in the E.R. Wipe down all the stainless in the main bays with Isopropyl. Empty out all the minor-surg sets from the autoclave and stack them in minor-surge bay. 17 y.o. girl. Comes in by ambo with apparent broken leg. She is in obvious discomfort, scared, and cooperative. I wheel her by gurney up to X-ray.

1700. Called to one of the upper floors to catheterize a middle-aged man who is post op, doing well, but still can't pee. He's tried and it's just not working. To make matters worse, he's got an IV drip going... and no place for all this fluid to go. Sometimes the anesthesia goofs up the machine for a while. He's a nice enough fellow, but I can see that he's struggling with the embarrassment and discomfort of the situation. I make jokes and tell him to relax while I quickly slip a small hose into his bladder. 1700 cc's of urine later, he's a smiling guy.

Back to the E.R. to assist Dr. Ravelli, the orthopedist, in the "break room." He's going to set the teenager's leg. Ravelli is a little pitbull of a man with thick forearms and a bald head. I'm short, but taller than Dr. Ravelli. I set out plaster rolls, basins of hot water, and check locks on the operating table, which has the ability to be broken apart in any way that is useful in setting limbs. He knocks the girl out with IV Valium, and has me brace her in a certain way. He yanks a bit here, and yanks a bit there, but he's not happy. He knocks away a part of the table and yanks a little more. The girl is a little chubby and slippery and escapes from my grasp. Ravelli yells at me, "Hold tight or you'll kill her, you fool!" I am pissed and embarrassed and renew my hold. Another snap and apparently he's satisfied and we set up the cast. I wheel her up to a recovery room still fuming from the stinging upbraid. When I get back to the nurses' station, I start bitching about how I'm not gonna work with Ravelli anymore. He slides up behind me and bearhugs me off the ground. "My little Mr. Rogers! Don't be mad with Ravelli. You know that I love you!! You are my second hands in the E.R.! I'm Italian! You know we are people with the hot blood! We only scream at the people we love!"

1830. supper. Peanut butter sandwich and a coke. I read half a chapter of sociology.

1900. Called to floors to "prep" two guys for surgery the next day. I hate "prepping." It means bathing and shaving large swaths of somebody's body. Sometimes entire abdominal and pubic areas...nobody is comfortable. It's embarrassing, and it's not easy to do. The razors can nick easily, especially upon skin that's not used to being shaved. I try to make barber small talk, but I really hate it.

2030. In the E.R., there's a crowd developing, and all the bays are filled. I slip into the routine of taking TPRs and putting people into bays as they empty. Just about everybody's got primary care complaints: sniffles, chills, and fevers. It's obvious that flu season is coming in early. All the docs and nurses are hustling, but none of it is really an emergency. Ursula, one of the night nurses pulling an early shift, gripes, "Obviously nothing good on TV tonight."

2200. Called to the morgue to meet an undertaker and transfer a body. A man who died on day shift has been lying on a cold litter in the cooler. This particular funeral director tends to drive his hearse alone and often picks up bodies at night. He says he is so busy during the day with "arrangements," and it's quieter at night to pick up bodies from the hospitals. He always slips me a silver dollar as a tip.

2330. Party going on at the TEKE house. Lots of drunk students packed into every possible space, drinking beer and listening to very loud music. Lots of Bowie. My old roommate from last year must be at the turntable. I am trying to look cool in my Dr. Kildare whites while too-quickly drinking some beers, trying to catch up with the social level of intoxication. There's a laughing girl in a corner who's not very impressed with me. She's a social welfare major. One day I will marry her.

Day One

It is my first day on my job after undergraduate school. I have just walked onto a locked ward at the Seriously Expensive Private psychiatric Hospital (SEPpH). Once inside the ward, I turn around to lock the door behind me.

A young man has padded quietly up behind me. "Adolf Hitler! Adolf Hitler! Adolf Hitler!" he screams. I unlock the door, quickly step outside, and lock the door again. Through the window of the door the young man has pressed his face and is still screaming at me: "Adolf Hitler! Adolf Hitler! Adolf Hitler!"

A tall, skinny, bearded nurse comes up behind me and takes out his key to unlock the door and escort me onto the ward. He leans into the window and looks through the window. "Step back from the door, Danny. We have to come into work." He smiles and pats me on the back. "Relax," he says to me, "that's Daniel. That's just his way of saying hello. He's got a kind of an authority thing goin'. You'll get the hang of it."

We step inside. The patient who has been screaming offers me his hand in welcome.

I take the hand and shake it.

A Damn Good Question

"No, seriously man."

"This is not paranoia. This the fifth hospital I've been in. Where do they get all this green paint? Somebody's makin' all this paint. There's got to be a reason. Why all the walls always so damn green?"

Angry?

I am a first-year social work student.

The man on the third floor post surgical ward lay with his face to the wall. It had been five days, the nurses indicated, since his surgery, and that was the way he laid every day. He was not talking. He was not eating. He was not cooperating with his postsurgical care. He refused to get up and make efforts at walking. He was passive and largely uncommunicative. They knew he was conscious and alert, as he grudgingly participated in linen changing and bed baths. He had been gregarious and flirty before the operation, they said. He was a different man who had come back from the O.R.

He had worked for years as an able seaman on Great Lakes boats. According to his chart, he'd been diagnosed with some kind of abdominal cancer and had surgery to remove a tumor and had been given an ostomy bag[7] as a result of the surgery.

For two days in a row, I walked up to his bed and tried to engage him in a conversation. He just lay with his face to the wall.

Louise ran into me as I was writing a note. She asked me how things were going with Mr. Salter. I told her I wasn't quite sure, but he seemed very depressed. I discussed his lack of appetite, lethargy, and his lack of communication. I suggested maybe his situation was too severe for social work efforts and that perhaps a psych consult be requested. She nodded in a non-committal way, looked up and thought for a moment, and then asked me what I thought Mr. Salter was feeling. There she was going again, always looking for the feelings.

"I duuno," I replied, "the guy really hasn't talked with me. I think he's depressed and needs to see a psychiatrist." She looked at me in mock approval and said, "I understand. But if he isn't talking to you what magic is the psychiatrist going to have to allow him to talk with him?"

I was about to reply when she cut me off. Playfully, she asked me again about what I thought the patient was feeling. I rolled my eyes... "Oh, sad, I guess."

"Sad?" she said. "Are you sure? Sad? Do you really think he feels sad?"

"Yeah," I answered back. "I think he feels sad. He's just had big surgery. He's probably had a lot of pain. He woke up with a colostomy, and he mourns his regular ability to move his bowels. He probably feels sad."

She leaned into me. Locking me deep in the eyes. I watched her pupils flitter back and forth, really, really looking at my eyes. "Hmm. Sad?" she said again. "I'm not sure you are really using your empathy. Empathy is the most important tool in the social worker's toolbox. It's like a flashlight to help you find your way. Mr. Salter has had a lot of losses. If you were in his shoes, would you feel sad?"

"Sure. Yeah." I muttered back. "Sad."

She leaned in further still. She seemed to tower over me. Still, she was probing with her eyes. "Sad?" she repeated, "When you think about it now, do you really feel sad? Do you feel sad? If you woke up with a colostomy and I was talking with you like you were talking with him, would you feel sad? Is that what you would feel? Are you sure?"

I flustered, "I... I... I..." My face was flushing. I knew as I could feel the heat pumping through my temples.

"What do you feel?" she stared deeper. She cocked her head like a dog. "Right now?"

I choked and then balled my fists. I could feel myself sputtering. "Louise...I feel pissed right now. I feel pissed 'cause you're always questioning about how I feel." My voice was rising, "I feel pissed because...."

Cutting me off with a wave, she snapped upright and raised a cautioning hand toward me. She smiled quietly and scrunched her face with an inquiring look. "Pissed," she said still smiling, "I think you're on to something there!" And she turned on her heel and briskly walked away.

I fumed quietly to myself for a little while. I sat and shook my head and wondered to myself why she was always making me feel crazy. Then I thought about Mr. Salter. Perhaps she was right. I was wrong about how the patient was probably feeling. The guy was probably not sad...he was probably pissed.

The next day, I approached Mr. Salter's bed, again standing at the foot of it. I took a moment to look at his position. As had been typical for the past few days, he was curled up beneath his blankets, facing the wall. I took a look at the nursing chart at the foot of the bed and then replaced it. I started slowly. I leaned over the side of the bed.

"You know, I want to apologize to you. I've been comin' here for the past couple days, comin' to see you and sayin' how sad you must be, an' can I help...but it dawned on me that I've been way off base. You're probably not sad at all. You're probably pretty angry, I figure. I'm sorry I've been wastin' your time. I'm sorry I've been saying you're sad when you're probably just pissed."

I didn't have the period on my sentence when he whipped up and around to the side of the bed. He sat bolt upright and leaned out and grabbed me by the lapels of my little white lab coat. Given his post surgical status, I was startled by his agility and found myself frozen.

"Pissed!? You think? Angry? Me? Angry?! You think?!" He tightened his grip upon my coat. "How can I get angry? Who can I get angry with? I'm laying like a baby in this bed, with my butt hangin' outta this sh**ty gown. I can barely bathe or feed myself I'm in such pain. Can I get angry at the nurses? Hell, no! They're the ones feedin' me. Can I get angry at the docs? They got this hole in my belly drainin' sh*t into a plastic bag. I can just wait to see me trying to lay with a woman with this sh**ty thing stickin' outta me. Can I get angry at them? Hell no! If it weren't for those f***ers cutting the tumor outta me, I'd probably be worse off! What about God? Howabout Him? Can I blame him for getting this sh**ty cancer in the first place? Did he give me that f***in' tumor the size of a baseball in my guts? Can I get angry at Him? Hell no... If I did, what else is he gonna throw at me?! Lightning bolts?!"

"Angry?! I'm so f***in' angry I could scream. What did I do to deserve this? I'm so f***ing angry I'm gonna get outta this hospital, buy me a 45-caliber pistol, a ticket to the Navy-Notre Dame football game, and blow my f***in' brains out on the fifty-yard line at halftime. I'm sure as sh*t angry...but who can I get angry at?"

I looked down at his fists on my lapels. Then I looked him in the eyes. "Well, I guess, we can start with me."

He eyed me up and down. He released me from his grip. "OK," he said. "We can start there."

3 a.m. SEPpH

I am sitting in the day room in the middle of the night. B-4 is a long hall with a large number of patients at the long established Seriously Expensive Private psychiatric Hospital (SEPpH). Everyone is asleep.

I am reading *The Skills of Helping*, by Shulman,[8] and am at a place where he discusses reaching for the "authority theme" in relationships. I hear the faintest jingle of keys, which slowly grows louder. I know that it is Winston, a nurse from Trinidad, who is working this night shift with me.

He plunks himself down on a nearby couch and cradles a cup of coffee.

"Winston, my man, I can hear you coming a mile away."

He smiles. "If you know where I am, you can know where I am not. You can choose to be good or bad. It is best to be bad where I am not, and good where I am."

I looked up at him from my book. "Winston, you are a Buddha."

2 a.m. SEPpH

I was writing notes late on the ward.

"Psssst," she said, all of about 80 years, 90 pounds, tiny, white-haired, wrinkly, and giggly. Strapped into the geri-chair and wide-awake in her manic effervescence, a wild woman's grin lighting up the otherwise silent hallway. She and I, the only ones awake on the ward.

"Psssst." She winked, and beckoned I sit closer.

"It's okay if you want. I won't tell anybody," she began.

"What's that?" I asked.

"It's okay. There's nobody around." She giggled again.

"What's okay?" I leaned closer, smiling, a grandmother transference enveloping me.

"You can pet my Suzie." She smiled. "It's okay. I won't tell anyone."

I straightened just a bit in my seat. "Well, I'm flattered, Mrs. Wiener...."

"It's okay. I'd like it. I won't tell anybody."

I continued, "...but it's against hospital policy."

She giggled. "They're all asleep. Nobody will know," she continued her seduction.

"Ethel," I scratched my head, "I hear you, but we just can't. It's against the rules. I think it's better if we just be friends."

"If you were my friend, you'd pet my Suzie." She winked at me again.

"Then I'll just have to be your worker."

She frowned a moment, and then beamed at me again. "I'm a hottie," she said.

I went back into the office to resume my notes. "On that, Ethel," I said, "we agree."

Addiction

Driving home after my second afternoon of comprehensive examinations, I am stopped by the light at W. Lexington and Paca. It is cold, gray, and windy. What had been a misty sleet was beginning to turn to flurries. The windshield wipers made their usual rhythmic thump. With the red light in the distance, exhausted, spent from two days locked in a little room writing essay after essay, I was numb and found only enough interest to watch the mixture of droplets and ice crystals fall onto my car's window. The walk to the garage had been bitter as I had not dressed for inclemency. It was only now, at the intersection, could I feel the warmth filling the interior of my automobile, the chill receding from my body.

I focus out the driver's side and notice him. He is tall and thin and black, and standing with a shaking side-to-side shuffle trying to keep warm. He's only wearing a hoodie, and the shoulders have darkened from the wet. He wipes his eyes and nose and hyperscans the horizon. It seems obvious that he is miserable and waiting. Waiting for the man. Waiting for the man and carrying his kid. Asleep, his doll's head wobbling to the rhythm, a baby hunches in the papoose on his father's back. They are both waiting for the man.

The light turns green, and I put my car into gear. As I turn into the intersection, I look up again and look at him. He has looked at me, and for a few brief moments we are locked into each other's gaze, both of us looking at the other with eyes that reveal nothing. A few blocks up Paca Street, I am stopped at another light, and without warning, uncontrollably, I begin to sob. The crying lasts a couple of blocks more as I make my passage home. I am startled at myself and have no notion of from where this pathos sprung. Bone weary, I drive on, puzzled, as I am not one to weep easily.

Almost home, I begin to consider what we will do for supper. I consider the leftovers I remember in the fridge. I consider the tastes of my wife, and my first and second born. Then it dawns on me that like the fellow on the corner, I too have an infant child. I have an infant child who I have not been tending well to in these last months. So busy working and going to school. So busy immersed in the classroom and the books and the study. I didn't need to work on this last degree; it was a luxury of joining others in the rarified air of the ivory towers. I wanted more school because I loved it, and it stimulated me in a way that I was missing from my patients. I loved school because I was good at it and enjoyed the bon-homme of talking theory with my friends, the good doctoral candidates.

As I pulled up to the curb, it was still snowing a wet, heavy snow. The porch light showed the path to the house, and my family, warm inside. I understood now my tears, and how the man on the corner and I were more alike than different.

Accommodation of a Paradigm Shift

It was my first real job after grad school—a position as a clinician in a full spectrum Department of Psychiatry in a large general hospital. One of the things I did for the Department was cover the hospital emergency department. Now I was the fellow who was going to interview the behaviorally presenting patients, making the call for admission to the hospital or the state hospital up the road, or triaging the patient to the outpatient department for the next day's appointment.

She was a petite 40-something dressed in silver satin hotpants and a tube top. She wore two huge security guys from the "American Engineering Company in the Middle East" on both wrists. She was absolutely effervescent, flirting with me and the security guys (who after 19 hours on planes with her looked pleadingly at me to end their assignment). She was married to an engineer, and her behavior was causing a scandal back in some Arabian country.

She flitted from subject to subject in response to all of my questions, often going from idea to idea without using any periods in her sentences. My goodness! It was true! She hadn't slept for three days! She just laughed and laughed, and told me how silly a little old thing like sleep was:

"Butwhoneedssleepanywaytheresjustsomuchneatstuffgoinonand-canIgetadrinkandlookatthisnewringmyhusbandboughtitsadiamon-dandtheyarejustsoshinyohIprobablyneedtopowdermynose..."

She agreed to voluntary admission to the inpatient unit. She said she hadn't taken any medication in months.

After conferring by phone with the supervising psychiatrist, I sat in the back of the nurses' station writing orders for her admission on the unit: Diet, privileges, admission lab work, referrals. Larry would call in meds as soon as she was seen by one of the internal medicine residents. I was happy that for my first admission to the inpatient unit, it was just a slam-dunk for a diagnosis and she had been so cooperative on voluntary admission.

I was trying to look my most professional. There was this charge nurse on the unit that I was trying to impress. "Well," I said to the assembled nurses, "let's get this happy little lady settled in. We oughta be able to chill this mania in a couple of months."

The head nurse snickered. "Honey, you'll get this patient leveled out in 10 to 15 days, or you'll be back in grad school."

"But Mrs. Wilson," I protested (probably a little officiously), "I've seen dozens of manic patients treated at the Seriously Expensive Private psychiatric Hospital...I worked for years at SEPpH. It always takes at least a couple of months to diminish mania."

"You're in community mental health now, Honey. Nobody has 'couple of months' insurance. I'm tellin' ya, in and out in 15 days."

The patient stabilized and transferred to outpatient care 12 days later. It was a crack in my cosmic egg.[9]

Why not Why

I sat down across from the elderly gentleman. According to the consult form, he was suffering from depression. I introduced myself and my role as the social worker from the behavioral health service, sent at the request of his physician at the long-term care center. He nodded slowly.

"So," I asked, "Why do you think you are feeling this way?"

He shook his head. "Oh, no. That's no way at all to begin."

"I'm sorry?"

"No, you're not sorry. But that's not the point. You never want to start off with 'Why.' 'Why' is static and requires a static answer. 'Why' connotes a responsibility on my part that makes just a greater burden of judgment upon me in relationship to you. I would not want to start that way. Feeling judged. Feeling that a difficulty somehow resides within me. Additionally, just how useful will the answer really be to either of us? I may have some sense of the causation of my difficulties, but it will be just one perception of what surely must be a multifaceted problem, and even if I was that sure of that causation, of what use would be the additional consultation with you then? No, 'why' is just a terrible way to begin. I think a 'what' or 'how' would yield a much better process. A more dynamic orientation to a dynamic exploration."

I looked closely at him. "No. I really am sorry. You are absolutely correct. Let me begin again. I'm Mr. Rogers. Am I correct in assuming that you are Mr. Thornton?"

"Actually, It's Smith-Thornton, and it's Doctor. I hold a Ph.D. in linguistics."

"I am pleased to meet you Dr. Smith-Thornton. I must tell you that I sincerely believe that I will look forward to this conversation. I would like to know more about how you are feeling today."

"Ah, much improved," he said. "I suspect you will be a good social worker."

"How is that?" I asked.

He smiled a little. "Well, I feel better already."

Experience of the Other: The Case of Taboo and Metaphor

Mrs. Stollfust sat in the same chair every Thursday at 10:00 a.m. She was smallish for the typical Berks County, Pennsylvania, farm wife, a job she had occupied almost her whole life. Referred by her local family doctor, I had known her for about six months. Her presenting problem had been a mixed picture of complaints about anxiety and blue mood. Her husband, Vernon, had died a number of years earlier and she "had yoost never got back on her feet." She lived with her adult daughter, Anna, who worked in a car dealership in Shillington.

Mrs. Stollfust and I had settled into a fairly common clinical routine. She had been resistant to coming to the mental health center, her only medical professional being the "doktor" she had known in her little town for years. He, however, was uncomfortable with treating "nervous disorders" for more than a few months, and after some weeks of vague complaints about various pains, Mrs. Stollfust had just burst into tears in his office and protested that life was no longer worth living. Our relationship had begun in the hospital emergency room at his insistence. Since then, she had grown to trust me to be a good listener, and knew me as the "social worker who verks mit da nerve doktor." In the CMHC where I worked, I was responsible for her case, and we had a psychiatrist who had prescribed an antidepressant medication upon my request for a pharmacology evaluation.

She was a pleasant enough woman, if not unlike a number of similar clients I had at the time. She was fairly concrete, not one to spend much time looking inside her feelings or thoughts, and had a fairly classic picture of a "biological" depression. After some period of assessment, the time we spent together each week had been at first organized around the importance of taking her medication, support around side effects, and supportive encouragements about her "nerves getting better."

Over the months, we had slowly expanded our conversations to include the various minor problems in her daily life, which was a largely isolated one, and considering vaguely the possible solutions, which usually had some frustration to their possibility. I had tried to see if I couldn't get her to start adding some social activities to her routine, but she hadn't been much of a social person most of her life, and had signaled me that she wasn't inclined to change now. Her symptoms slowly but surely remitted, after the usual side effect difficulties that came at first. The tears had stopped, her anxiety had diminished, appetite picked up, sleep got better, and the suicidal thought had been chalked up to "chust plain foolishness." I was at the point of soon discussing tapering her weekly visits to a more distant sequence, perhaps monthly. She was rapidly falling into that category of "medication monitoring patients" that each of the clinicians had on their caseload. Pleasant folks. Nice enough. But, essentially, in remission of symptoms, offered little psychological content for a young "therapist" to do except learn more about the absence of "vegetative symptoms of depression" in remission.

In the later visits, the patterns of our conversation had become so fixed that I came to interact in a pleasant, caring, "autopilot." After taking a brief history, I pronounced that her nerves sounded "almost all better," to which she agreed and then would accommodate me with a report of the various trivial things that had occurred during the week. It was usually a laundry list of small frustrations that she would first profess, and then quickly minimize. I would nod or offer the mildest encouragement, and she would go on with some small details, minimize some more, then wander off about some other banal frustration. This would last about 35 minutes or so, and then she would look at her watch, look squarely satisfied at me, and pronounce how I and the medication had obviously been helping her. I would agree and then take another moment to schedule another appointment.

Pleasant enough. Dull. Meat-and-potatoes community mental health. I had other patients with more demand and challenge. I had relegated Mrs. Stollfust to autopilot of my attentions.

It was halfway into this week's litany that I was shocked out of my half-listening stance. There had been nothing out of the pattern of the presentation she had manifested for weeks. We were having a pleasant give-and-take about some of life's minor aggravations. She had just rattled off a small list when she came to a summation, "And on top off all dat, my daughter fell off da roof!"

Somewhat taken aback by the nonchalant pronouncement of what sounded like a potentially fatal accident, I sat bolt upright and blurted back, "Oh my goodness! Was she badly hurt?"

Mrs. Stollfust, now mirroring my surprise, retorted, "Why, no! Why I never heard such a thing!" I was stuck with a vision of her daughter lying helpless in the yard. "Well, did you call an ambulance!?" Mrs Stollfust looked at me in horror, "I vould nefer do dat!" Shocked, I was stunned by this woman who was showing me a side I never imagined. I groped for a comment. "I don't understand, Mrs. Stollfust...she's your daughter!"

The patient was clearly upset by my urgency. She sputtered and primped angrily, clearly frustrated and confused with me. Abruptly, she stood and made for the office door. "That vill do enough already!" She barked, "I will go... Now!" She stomped down the hall while I sat puzzled and confused.

Some hours later that day, I was having lunch with a good colleague discussing the odd event that occurred with this patient I thought I knew fairly well. I expressed my alarm over the situation, especially how the session had so chaotically dissolved. When he asked me what about the client had so shocked me, I told him.

"Well, here's this sweet little old lady I've been treating for anxiety and depression. She's been getting better, actually...soon to be put into a monitoring pattern. I've worked with her for about six months. Anyway, today she's reciting the usual stuff of day-to-day life and then recounts that her daughter had a terrible accident on the farm and she did utterly nothing to assist."

"How old's the daughter?" my colleague asked.

"About late 30s," I replied.

"What happened?" he asked further. "She fell off the roof of the house," I answered.

"The roof of the house?" he asked, "or just fell off the roof?" I was peeved. "What's the difference?" I asked.

"Well," he said, laughing gently. "If she fell off the roof of the house, she could've broken her back, but if she just 'fell off the roof,' that's a euphemism for getting her period, and maybe she was cranky with her mom."

I called the client to apologize and explain my misunderstanding. Ever since, I've been more careful about jumping to conclusions.

The Sharp Edge of Theory

For reasons I don't want to get into, I abandoned psychosocial theory. Well, at least the psychodynamic theory of psychosocial theory.

I was surprised that the case was assigned to me, as the presenting problem was so clearly defined as a phobia in a middle-aged woman. When I pointed out that this was not my usual expertise of practice, the triage officer (who was the head of the psychology department) indicated that: "1) the patient lived with her elderly mother (and I was perceived as the agency's 'gerontologist'), 2) he would personally provide me with supervision on the case, and 3) none of the psychologists on staff had time to take on any new patients." It seemed the matter had been settled.

The patient was a 49-year-old female who lived alone with her invalid mother. She was mildly depressed and anxious. Increasingly, over the last six months, she had become anxious when she would go into the kitchen to prepare a meal, and noticed that she would tremble when she would pick up a knife during cooking. This fear had steadily increased to the point that she was now having panic attacks every time she walked into the kitchen and was getting into terrible arguments with her mother, as the both of them had been reduced to eating cereal for just about every meal. The patient was insistent that she had become afraid of knives and that the merest mention of, or even thinking about, knives was causing her to panic.

In the interview, I found (or perhaps I really did not find!) that I had become so focused on the phobia of knives, the apparent discreteness of the problem, and my own sense of inadequacy about how to "treat" a phobia, that I had failed to ask any of the other usual questions that were part of my initial interview. When I was doing my write-up at the end of the session, I found myself referring back to the triage paperwork to see if that patient had a job (she did, she worked in a clothing factory for many years), how much education she had (high school graduate), or any other supports (according to the paperwork, "none").

I consulted with the chief psychologist who spent about a half hour with me outlining a course of therapy based upon systematic desensitization theory. The psychologist had studied under Joseph Wolpe[10] at

Temple. He gave me a couple of articles on relaxation training techniques and an outline of how to proceed with a graduated exposure regimen. The theory seemed simple and straight-forward, and the psychologist explained that he and Wolpe had both had the same dissatisfaction with psychoanalytic theory, just like me (for reasons I won't go into) that had led them to this present behavioral based approach. It was perfect for phobia. Once the patient had mastered being able to induce relaxation, it would be impossible to experience anxiety. I would introduce very small and distant stimuli that were phobic while she was in the relaxed state, and then practice gradually making the stimuli larger, closer, and more real.

So, I saw the patient twice a week for five weeks. I outlined how I planned to approach her knife phobia, and she agreed. She mastered relaxation techniques easily in two weeks. By week three, I started simply saying the word "knife," while she induced relaxation. She felt in control and pleased with herself. In the next session, I had a picture of a scout knife in the corner of my office, which I made no reference to. She practiced relaxation. I called her attention to the picture and asked her to continue practicing relaxation. She did so and was pleased with herself. The next session, I put a little scout knife on my desk and made no reference to it. She practiced relaxation. I called her attention to it and asked her to continue practicing. She did so and was pleased with herself. I asked her if I could move the knife off the desk and onto the table between us. She agreed and kept on practicing. I asked about her anxiety. She said she was feeling a little, but it was good anxiety, not a fear of knives anxiety. She was feeling in control, and she liked it.

In the sessions over the next few weeks, we continued the increasing exposure and the relaxation practice. We got to the point that we practiced in the clinic kitchen. She touched knives while relaxing, and we even cut up some veggies and made a salad. We used some big knives! We cut celery, lettuce, tomatoes, carrots, and onions. She laughed. When I asked her how she was feeling, she said, "Wonderful! I think I'm cured. I can't thank you enough!"

I reported the case to the psychologist, and he agreed we could discuss closing the case if the patient had no more concerns. She agreed. She said she felt great.

That Friday evening, I got a call to come down to the E.R. My patient needed assessment for admission to the psych unit. The resident said my patient was suicidal.

When I got to the E.R., there was my patient, lying on a gurney with both arms completely bandaged. The chart indicated she had multiple lacerations that required dozens of stitches. She was crying, a blubbering, miserable creature. When I asked why she had tried to kill herself, she just broke down in huge sobs.

"I wasn't trying at first. I went into the kitchen to make some supper. I started chopping some celery and then I got to thinking about how I didn't want to make supper for my mother. It was Friday night, and I wanted to go out and not be so lonely. I want to meet a man and have a boyfriend. I hate living with my mother. But what am I going to do? Someone has to take care of her. I thought for the slightest of a second how I could kill my mother. I was horrified of that thought! What a horrible daughter I am. That's when I realized I should just kill myself. I had the knife in my hand and just started slicing away. I started bleeding all over, and it hurt so much I called an ambulance. I'm a terrible person. I just want to die."

I admitted her into the unit. Over the course of the next several weeks, we talked deeply and extensively about her life. Her problems, goals, and possible solutions.

For reasons I just went into, I renewed my appreciation of psychosocial theory. Well, at least the psychodynamic theory of psychosocial theory. Heck, a lot of psychosocial theory. I didn't throw behaviorism out with the bathwater, but I never let my theory get in the way of the client again.

Allison and the Role Theory

We were the "young turks" of the community mental health center, Allison, Mike, and me. Hanna hung with us, but we recognized already that he was the "zen master." Mike and Allison were an item and lived together...but everyone loved Allison.

Each day at 11 a.m., the staff convened in a conference room for the "Triage Meeting." The Triage Meeting's purpose was to introduce all the new cases that had presented to the agency the day before and to assign the responsibility of a case to a therapist for follow-up and treatment. Everyone on the staff took a turn at being the "Triage Officer," meeting with people or collateral referral sources, either in person or over the phone, doing initial assessment on new patients and crises that presented to the mental health center and the emergency room of the hospital.

There was a long conference table. Typically, whoever had been triage officer the day before sat in the middle and read the cases and briefly provided an initial assessment. As each of us at the agency had a sort of agreed upon "expertise," the decision as to who would pick up a case was often voluntary depending on the various qualities of the case. Allison usually took children. Mike tended to take marital cases. I was recognized as the geriatrician and also took persons with chronic and persistent mental illness. Hanna often took the adolescents. And so on, around the table everybody was usually amiable about taking their share of the new cases as they were presented.

At one end of the table sat the Chief of Social Work; at the other sat the Chief of Psychology.

For reasons lost to history long ago, the Chief of Social Work had abandoned any effort at leadership of the triage meeting...so the Chief of Psychology had become the person of last decision. On occasion, no one would volunteer for a case that had just been presented. Either the case sounded complex, hopeless, litigious, or just a whole lot of work, or the agreed upon "expert" had already taken what they thought was their share of cases that day. At such times, the Chief of Psychology would assign the case to a therapist, who would usually gripe and moan for a little bit, but then acquiesce and take the case.

This made the Chief Psychologist "the bad guy," and for the angels of their lesser natures, people would tend to resent him. I'm sure he picked up on the little resentments, and he developed an "attitude" over time that was sort of officious, arrogant, and marginalizing.

Well, it came to pass that the Chief Psychologist resigned from the mental health center to take a job in private practice. This meant a new Chief Psychologist would need to be appointed. The Chief Psychiatrist took some time to think about it, and on Friday announced that Allison would be appointed to the job.

We young turks were ecstatic! The torch had been passed to a new generation, and it would be our beloved Allison! We all went out to our favorite watering hole and celebrated the new future that awaited.

Over the weekend, five new cases came in and were to be presented by the triage officer as we sat down to the Monday morning meeting. Allison took her new seat at the end of the table. She was dressed as she usually was in a conservative, yet sharply cut, business suit. What shocked us was her behavior, speech, and personality—all of her decisions, all of her speech, all of her mannerisms were exactly similar to the man who had sat in the chair the week before! Around the table we sat, stunned, with our mouths open. Allison had become a *bitch!* She was defensive, authoritarian, and non-negotiable. We were shocked. Our lovely sweet Allison. We couldn't believe it.

At lunch, I asked Hanna what he thought.

Between bites of tuna sandwich, he remarked, "I think Erving Goffman[11] is a genius."

On Wearing My Tie

Being human, I court paradox and inconsistency. No one who knows me would ever think me careful about the way I dress. What has been wonderful about the life of the undergraduate academic social worker is that I am suitably attired in jeans and cottons and sneakers, except for the occasional visit to the Provost that might require slacks and cordovan shoes. A smallish, plumpish, whitish male, I have grown happy becoming careless in my costume. A study in rumpledness and comfort. I have flannel in winter, cotton in summer, and wrinkles all about. But they are comfortable wrinkles.

In my mind's eye, I am a taut terrier of 22. The sort of boy who was quick witted and self assured in class, but just shy enough to be vulnerably attractive to various sisters of the Phi Beta Mu house. My vision is dispelled each morning in the shaving mirror as I must confront what I really am: a dinner roll—soft, yeasty, and with a bit of stale crust. I throw my clothes on easily as I prepare for the day. I'm sure I've worn the same shirt two days in a row at least once. I will never be on the cover of *GQ*. I just don't think about how I dress.

That is not to say I am unmindful of social responsibility. I have a blue blazer for the odd job search or paper to present at a conference. I am careful to take a yarmulke to a synagogue, green socks to Boy Scout camp. I wear Maryland's hood at the springtime commencement. I don't want to offend when I am a guest, and so I am respectful of dressways and folkways of invited occasions. I will seek counsel from my spouse: "What should I wear?"

And that is not to say that I don't have a few vanities about my appearance. I do wear some jewelry. I have a small simple wedding band on my left hand that I never take off, as I am sure I would float off the earth and die. Each morning, I put my college ring on my third finger, right hand. It is one of those absurdly huge, Josten's golden oak knots of a ring that has always been far too big for my stubby little hands. My pinky has grown deformedly isolated from its mates over the years, the price I pay in homage to my alma mater—that wonderful time of youth dancing with adulthood. On the left collar of my shirt, I stab a very small Greek red cross surrounded in a circle of white. A beauty mark for a man who died a hundred years ago.[12] The curious who ask about it are sure to hear more from me than they expect. I wear a watch. It is a simple analog Timex favored by nurses. I had a digital one once, but I could not make my mind count a wrist pulse and read numbers at the same time. Its plastic crystal is scratched.

But, about the tie....

I am fastidious about wearing it.

I don't own many, and they are all about the same. Dark, simple woven cotton thinnish ties that are square on their bottom. I can't buy them anymore as no one sells them. I can't abide the wide, gaudy billboards of present fashion, and the peacock salesmen of the menswear world stare blankly at me when I show them mine and ask if they have any like it. But each morning, I am careful when I knot it around my collar.

There is nothing comfortable about my tie. Therein lies my inconsistency. It is functionless adornment, as my shirt has good buttons. I will not get cold without it. It's potentially dangerous. It can get caught in machines, and more than once, a desperate human has grabbed it and pulled me down to the ground.

My father wore these skinny little clip-on bow ties every day when he went to work that made him look shorter than the short he really was. I can remember a conversation at thirteen with Alonso Best as we rode our bikes through northwest Baltimore. "Man, I ain't never gonna get no job where I gotta wear a tie!"

My first day at my first placement, USPHS Hospital-Baltimore, I wore a tie. I wore it, I am sure, as I did not want to offend my social work supervisor. I wore it because I had been warned by my field liaison to be "dressed professionally" for a hospital. I probably wore it because I was afraid and excited and I thought I could hide behind it. I have worn one to work ever since. For me, the tie has become the vestment of profession. A commitment to the day, that today, I will be a social worker. I am reminded of an old Episcopal catechism: "An outward and visible sign of an inward and spiritual grace." I don my tie much like a priest might don a stole. I am but a person, but I will for this day be something just a little larger than myself. There is a grace to social work. In its heart there is a quiet reward that comes from the struggle of having faith with its ethics. More than once, I have lost sleep in some conflict with "client self-determination" and the power of apparent forces. Yet, also more than once in the quiet of an evening, I have counted the blessings that have come from my keeping true to some professional ethic, even when it made no sense to me in the moment. If I have married also social work, my tie has become a symbol of my vow. She has demanded much from me, yet also grounds me to the earth.

My ties have been "too skinny" to hide behind. The authority of the social worker cannot shield the will that is weak. I have had to grow into my tie over the years. There is no magic that prevents me from making mistakes or having faults to my courage. My tie is not invincible, like Superman's cape. But it does have a strength that I have drawn from in my fragile moments.

I often think of my personal self, which "lies beneath the tie," and the self that is professional, and how one lives with the two. I have found myself clutching my tie when the devils of my weaker nature arise—the client whose fantastic story might provoke the voyeur that dwells within, the client whose physical attractiveness calls upon the fantasy of my libido, the client whose utter helplessness raises my fear of failure, the client whose horrible behavior calls forth a bile in the back of my throat. Each comes to me for help and requires protection from me. The tie reminds me of who I am, and yet who I also profess to be. It is my contract with my colleagues and my society. An outward and visible symbol of my inward commitment to this social work.

My few ties have grown somewhat ratty and "seasoned" over the years. A little soup here, a spot of gravy there. Yet, there are stains also of tears, compassion, and strength. Crumbs of joy, sadness, and perseverance. My ties have developed "character" in their daily use around my neck. I will wear one every day as I walk to the agency. I wear each with pride and humility, for beneath the tie I am both me, and a social worker.

Stuck in a Loop. Reboot With Hope and Chaos.

His parents found him sweating and frantic, pushing around the refrigerator in the kitchen. He wouldn't stop and was brought to the psych unit in handcuffs. Three weeks later, he was to be discharged to home and to return to high school. The Haldol apparently had blunted him significantly.

When I got the case for outpatient follow-up, the child and adolescent psychiatrist said, "Work with the parents to get them to understand the kid is schizophrenic and has a chronic illness. Help the kid adjust to a simplified regime at high school."

I tried to be diplomatic. "Chris," I was tentative. "The kid's only 17. We've only seen him for three weeks, and two of them have been pretty medicated...he doesn't meet the criteria just yet for schizophrenia, no?"

He looked down the hall, somewhere above and beyond my head. "The kid's a schizophrenic. Just get them all settled down to simple expectations." And he walked off.

I met the kid and the parents three days later. The parents were in grief about a broken child who had been their pride—an "A" student who was an acolyte in their church, an Eagle Scout, by all their accounts, a brilliant driven young man who had no friends and tinkered endlessly with personal computers (a new machine at the time). There were plans for him to go to MIT, possibly early. Now, they were struggling with the unknown of a future with the limits of a serious and persistent mental illness. They worried about their younger daughter. Would she become ill, too? The kid said he couldn't focus in school. He was always falling asleep. He was drooling.

They wanted answers for all the fears from me.

I was supportive, but I wanted to introduce some breathing room into this crisis. "Sometimes, we need to get a bigger picture about things before the hospitalization, and how things have been since the hospital." I said I would like to meet with the parents alone, and the kid alone, and would have the kid seen by another psychiatrist, as now that he was an outpatient, we would have to use another doctor. (We really didn't "have to," but I didn't even think Chris would notice I didn't put the kid on his outpatient list. I would have the kid seen with me by Pete, an older and wiser psychiatrist with whom I shared a better professional relationship.)

Pete agreed we could slowly taper back on the medication, so the kid could perform more alertly in school. But the titration downward on the dose would depend upon me having a close relationship with the kid. As the high school was just a few blocks from the clinic, I gave him appointments on Tuesdays and Fridays right after classes. I saw his parents on Monday evenings.

What emerged quickly was a picture of a family with high personal expectations for one another, deeply seated orthodox religious faith, expansive intelligence amongst all the members, and boundaries that were just a little too close. While loving, the parents could be brutally punishing emotionally. Father was a somewhat imperious figure who could be quite challenging, and was extremely angry and frustrated by his son becoming "disabled."

The kid had an adolescence that lacked any real peer involvement. Even as a Boy Scout, he had tended to be a loner and just sailed through the requirements. I don't believe the word had been coined in terms of how it is used today, but mostly he was kind of a "computer geek." He was used to always following the rules. He was worried about going to college and being even more by himself without his parents. He was worried about getting straight A's. He was worried that he was always working and never really having fun. He was worried he didn't have a girlfriend. He was worried he couldn't talk to girls. One day, as it was warm and sunny, I told him we would have our session in the park outside the hospital. He worried about if that would be okay with the insurance company. He was worried about a lot.

One session, we talked about the night that landed him in the hospital. I asked him about the refrigerator deal.

"I was just so miserable that I wanted to die," he said. "But I couldn't commit suicide, because that's a sin and my parents wouldn't be able to bury me in consecrated ground. That would just kill them. I got stuck in a loop about all of this and decided that if I pushed the refrigerator around hard and long enough, I could give myself a heart attack, and then I could end everything, but everybody would still be okay."

So you probably have figured out where this case had to go.

I worked with the parents on Mondays to reach into a sense of hope for their son not to be seen as a broken thing, but a stronger bone that happens with the mending. We spent time talking about the need for a senior year in high school to have some opportunities for autonomy, for having some social experiences, for, ye gods, making some mistakes. We took it slowly; I didn't drop the mistakes theme right up front. But we examined their pride and got them to wrap their minds around the idea that for their little boy to become a genius, we needed to give him some permission to practice being a man.

On Tuesdays and Fridays, the kid and I talked about how to have fun without breaking into the rigid loops of sin and despair. We started out easy. I asked him to drive me out to the mall one day and asked him to drive two miles over the speed limit, as I was in a hurry. He smiled as we "broke the rules" and nobody got hurt. I smiled back. "I promise I won't tell your Dad."

We broke some other rules that senior year. Nothing really major or dangerous. Just little assignments of serendipity or secret little pleasures that he could have for just himself. We shared anxieties and strengths. I learned a lot more about computers. We talked about meeting girls. Yes, he even went to the prom.

All along, the medication came down to a point that there was no longer any on board. And months passed with no evidence of psychosis. Now don't get me wrong—even by graduation this kid was still one tightly wound rubber-band. But he had loosened, and his parents had loosened, just enough that when he went on to MIT, he wasn't stuck in a loop, and he wasn't a kid anymore.

P.S.: Yes, this one has a happy ending. Years later, with the help of an Internet search engine, I found out he went on to become a very successful software engineer who helped build an Internet search engine. He made lots of money and apparently has a family, and they have fun.

Building Wall

When the spring came, I had to build a wall. Over the winter, a builder had built a new house for my family. As the snows of northwestern Wisconsin receded, it became clear that the slope of the land would require a retaining wall to keep water away from the house.

The builder was really only interested in building houses. He did not want to build such a small wall as I desired. I asked the fellow who would do the excavating and grading of the land around the new house, but he was really only interested in moving and shaping earth with his large machines. He also did not want to build the small wall that I needed. I had occasion to discuss the matter with a landscape architect I had retained to look at the ground around my house and draw a plan of what plants and trees I might grow about it. He said that he would draw a picture of my wall, but it would be such a small wall that he was not interested enough to build it. He asked me what colors I liked.

So, it fell to me to build a wall. It would not be a big wall—perhaps five feet high at one corner of the house, and tapering along some twenty feet to a mere step.

After reading a little about walls, I decided to visit a mill where they made concrete blocks. I decided against building a wall from the complicated fitting of stone or serious masonry that might require the use of mortar. I had never built a wall before, and I did not want to bite off more than I could chew. I have never been a person who felt handy with his hands.

I also ruled out building the wall of wood. As much as I love wood, I feared it would rot over time and require repair. I was not fond of the idea of building this wall in the first place, and I could not invest in the contemplation of repairing it on some day in the future. The concrete people had done a lot of thinking about walls and they had come up with materials that could make a fine wall of a simple nature, holding soil to the slope I desired, and secured in its own weight.

The man at the concrete mill was a reassuring sort. He was kind to me and explained that despite my inexperience and anxiety over the matter, he had seen many people such as myself build very good walls. He patiently explained each step of building a wall using his concrete blocks, and he made me feel a little more confident. Strengthened by his care and wisdom, I went home to draw a plan of how big my wall would be, calculated the materials I would need, and arranged to have everything delivered.

Before the weekend commenced, the wall arrived on a big truck on three large pallets. The apparently simple matter remained to just take the pieces off the pallets and arrange them into my wall. "Not unlike playing with legos," I told my boys, who I enlisted to help me.

Rising early on a Saturday, I began to build the wall. It dawned on me quite early in the morning that building a wall has many of the qualities of learning to do social work, and as the day—excuse me, days—unfolded, this thought would recur often.

The first step of building a wall is the laying in of a proper foundation. A wide trench must be dug carefully, making sure that the first course of blocks will sit level, on a bed of locking stone gravel. It took me much longer than I thought it would to prepare this foundation. I had to dig a little more here, filling a little more there. Measuring, measuring, measuring. I laughed in frustration at one point, when looking down at two of the leveling measures I was using, both read differently. I considered my research students who struggled with the concepts of reliability and validity. In class and in the world, we struggled with such ideas as poverty, oppression, self-esteem, and empathy. Here I was merely trying to understand the nature of dirt and a straight line, and the bubbles in my levels appeared to defy what laws I thought were in nature. With time and much more effort, however, my foundation was complete. It foretold a solid base of crushed stone in a gently curving line that did not slope in any direction. Now I could build a wall.

The first course of the wall was nerve testing to build. Each block had to be nestled and tapped and placed just so right, so as to maintain the level that had just been so arduously carved into the earth. The blocks were heavy, about sixty pounds each. They would not just be banged about, but had to be carried respectfully and shifted artfully, each in its own right place, all in a right place with each other. I got angry when one would resist my measure. "Stupid block," I would curse, "why won't you just fit?!" Smacking them at that point did nothing except bruise my knuckles. I would wipe the sweat off my face and engage the misplaced block as a problem to be solved. "Work with me, block," I would whisper. "Where is the place that is not level?" "Let's find the place that you must fit." It was afternoon before the first course was done, and I could begin to build the wall.

After the first course of a wall is constructed level and tight, one must back fill it with pea gravel, and behind the pea gravel one must back fill with the soil that one wants to retain. It's a sneaky little fact, but the real backbreaking work of building a wall is in the shoveling, spade by spade, of all this gravel and soil. Dirt really doesn't seem all that heavy when it's just a shovelful. It's when it's hundreds of shovelfuls that it becomes work. Here I was, lucky to have the many hands of my young sons and their various cronies. Having sent them out into the neighborhood to borrow shovels, they now comprised the army of ants that filled in the back of the wall. The cost for such a resource was inexpensive: the suffering through of one waaaay too many pre-pubescent cracks about the urinary properties of pea gravel, and a couple of pitchers of KoolAid. Unlike myself, who was beginning to see this whole affair as much too much work, the 11-year-olds lined up in a playful competition with each other as to who could shovel faster. They were erratic and chaotic at first, running into each other and spilling soil into each other's shoes. But over time, they fell into a team-like rhythm, marching in a step that moved the hills of material many a spade at a time. I thought about the great wall of China and how working in concert many hands make vast work. I thought about what great energy there was in getting people to work in concert. How many can, if supported, move mountains. With the back fill building on each course, I could continue to build the wall.

My wife and I growled at each other at times over the course of the two days it took to build the wall. Straining against the draining strength of my middle-aged muscles, she would direct me to change an angle here, or place a wheelbarrow of soil there. I would snap angrily, focused as I was on my burden, not seeing the picture she was constructing of the problem she was solving about the wall. At such terse words, I would wonder if the wall was creating a wall between us, or whether such anger at what must surely be small frustrations was worth it. But before I might offer an apology, I would get a shovelful of dirt thrown against my butt...she could dish it out as well as take it. The angry snaps and the playful retorts had become the lime that quickens the mortar of our relationship. While we might be tested by the building of this wall, we would emerge more solid from the experience.

In the end, on a late Sunday afternoon, the wall was built. Behind it held a graceful slope of tons of soil. Its eastern face held open space and would catch the warming morning light of the sun. The rest of the week was filled with soaking rains and thunderstorms. The wall held and kept water away from the house. A friend of mine who is a construction supervisor, a man who builds Walmarts and Target stores across the U.S., stopped by. We had a beer in the backyard that still has so much work to do. He is a fellow of southern drawl and few words. "Good wall," he said.

So much of social work is making small things that so many will not notice. They will not be permanent, but the effects are important for those who are concerned. We will get little credit except from those who know the struggle and pleasure of plying our profession. "Good wall," he said, "It's work, to make a good wall." We sipped our beers and kept looking at it.

The poet Robert Frost once wrote, "Something there is that doesn't love a wall." He wondered about what forces tore apart the stone farm walls of Vermont in the quiet of wintertime and the warming of spring. I suppose there are good walls and bad walls. Walls that are well constructed for terrible purposes. Walls that are poorly built with the best of intentions.

A wall is like any boundary, and social workers should become the masters of boundary. We must learn to be the respectful nosey bodies. We must learn to be the nonjudgmental judges. We will walk along the places where pain and hope mix and mingle with strength and despair. We know that we walk in the spaces between. Perhaps sometimes we are the makers of walls, or lent to be walls ourselves. We must learn when to help others build boundaries between the "something there is" and the "something there isn't." We practice the building of good walls and the tearing down of troubles.

So, too, when I look out at the students who have passed in front of me, I can see that they are the builders of good wall. They struggle laying down that foundation. Shifting new ideas against the blocks of past beliefs. Tapping and molding the skills of empathy, reason, investigation, and action into a place where each will have a good fit. The blocks are heavy and frustrating to lift. And, it takes much, much more time to shape some of them than they forecasted. But when it is done, they come to know that whatever comes their way, they have built a strong place from which to begin—a boundary that can help them help the world.

I remember when I was in college, I read a book by a man named Studs Turkel. The book was titled *Working*,[13] and it detailed interviews with people about their jobs. I don't remember much of the book except that of the many jobs people discussed in it, only two people seemed to like their work. One was a firefighter and the other was a mason. I don't remember why the firefighter liked his work, except something about being a part of saving lives. What I remember about the mason was that he enjoyed the puzzle about thinking which stone should go where in a wall. He liked the color and the shape and the heft of what he worked with, and recognized that no wall ever stands forever. It was in the building of it that he enjoyed his work, not in some construction of a permanent future. In this academic year, which began with walls and firefighters collapsing like so much broken stone, I take some strength from that mason's perspective. What terrible walls have been built, that bring about so much rage as to fly an airplane into a building?[14] What good fences must be built to create a world with peace?

It will be the simple, yet difficult, work of building good foundations, of fitting each stone or block in the place that is just right. Of working with what we know in the moment, with what we don't know. Of considering how to be well, in between; of looking from both sides; of seeking a level. It will be heavy, but there are many hands who can join. And when we are done, it might not last forever, but it will be important, for those who will be most concerned. We can stand about, and sipping on a beer, look at it...and know.

2
Middles

Middles are places of hard work and confusion on one hand, and magic and transformation on the other.

I often think of social work as the practice of being-in or finding the middle. When problems are often secreted into the self, the social worker and the client work together to bring the problem out into the middle, where they both can see them. When the worker clearly articulates the services that the agency can provide, the client can be empowered to make choices about action. This can mean relief at one level, and a demand for work on the other.

In the social work relationship with a client, the middle is a time when the difficult effort of trying new tasks or engaging new thoughts meets with the friction of real practice. At the point of implementing new things comes anxiety and pain of exertion. One can think about ice skating as much as one wants—it's when one puts the blades on the ice that one glides, and falls, and gets up and tries to glide again.

Whole religious philosophies are about living in the middle, a place of being open to awareness of thought and feeling. The middle can be a place of terrific muddiness or great clarity. To have one, you have to have the other. That's what makes middles so wild. They are neither ends of beginnings or beginning of ends...they're, er, em, hmmm, middles!

In the Middle of a Middle

In mid life, midweek, mid April, in Midwestern America, I found myself thinking about middles. As a student, practitioner, and teacher of social work, I've approached the old practice chestnut, "beginnings, middles, and ends," what must now be thousands of times. In my life, I've paid so much attention to the outer boundaries so far. So much time and attention to the beginnings and ends. Lately, I think, the middles is what it's all about.

When I was a younger man, a student, I never really understood anything about middles. It was almost always about beginnings. The beginnings of relationships. The start of semesters. Initial interviews. The shock of the new in a world that was just unfolding for me. Much of my experience was always coming into confrontation with novelty: ideas, people, places, lovers, enemies. Life looms more vivid when things first begin. Images and smells and textures are charged with the inflorescence of anxiety. Buildings are taller. Eyes are more telling. The first views of things hold their shape in the mind's eye so much differently than when they appear in the later days of day-to-day.

When one is young, much of life is spent in anticipation. So much of what seems to be reality is really the conjuring of what will be. The moments of the present are filled with the expectation of the future— sometimes only minutes away. Indeed, preparation is such a way of being, that when things are in the swim of the moment, one can get surprised: "Oh, *this* is what it was supposed to be like!"

Social work was new to me, and my youthfulness charged hope into all the new endeavors I began. Sometimes there was no loss in this. I had clients who needed the extreme of my youth, and they borrowed hope upon the morrow. But there was tragedy when there was mismatch. When I had a vision that exceeded my clients' strengths, we needed to agree upon failures that could be measured as success. It is here that one gets into middles.

Likewise, "ends." Despite protestations of other writers, the ends of things get more attention than denial would suspect. Death abounds in the world, and there is more than enough awareness. We crane our necks at the highway wreck. The thoughts made taboo are the most important of all. They touch us frequently like an achy tooth that will not be forgotten. We tongue touch that tooth frequently, and knowing each time it will hurt, we persist.

Beginnings are filled with anticipation and hope. Ends are filled with the acuity of pain or joy, and memory. Middles, on the other hand, are duller places. Calms in the ocean of stormy relationships and problems. There is a familiarity. Difference is less acute, and therefore requires less agility. There is no motion on the water. What was once a stab is now the blunted ache, perhaps getting better, perhaps not. Vague silences that once provoked questions now become moments that just lack meaning and are filled with muddled confusions: Which way now? Forward or back? Fewer declarative sentences.

Middles of things are never well announced. They tend to sneak up upon one in, well, the middle of things. You note, for instance, one day, that there is a certain boredom in the room. There is a vague indifference that has entered into a glance up toward the wall. These are the hallmarks of a middle. The signs that an end is in the offing.

The writers of the Functional School of social work always had a great influence on me. I think it was Ruth Smalley[1] who made me dread middles. I had come to expect them as confusing and sullen times. I think Jessie Taft once wrote that there weren't really any middles; just the beginnings, beginnings of ends, and ends. Yet in describing the beginnings of ends, she found herself in the middle. Middles have a sense.... The client and I both bored with each other. The hope and expectations of goals that once seemed bright, yet small and far away, were now possibly quite closer, but somewhat dimmed in their development—grayer and perhaps dented.

Compromises are what really come to be. They are never sought in the beginnings of things. They are the bread of what really happens.

There are times now, in these days of the "end of history," that I see it seems to be difficult for people to tolerate the middle of things. It seems funny that in the dissolution of the Cold War when the world was divided into the two past worlds of east and west, people now seem more polar to me than ever before. So much of public discussion has become extreme to me. "Fundamental" and "radical" seem unresolvable at the very outset of a discussion. It seems as if the desire to search for the middle is lost.

Here is a place for the social worker. We are the people of the middles.

Social work is always about being in the middle. We are always guests in another's house. The social worker in the hospital is the one who knows most about outside of the hospital. The health care worker on the street is the person who knows most about getting into the hospital. The genius of the social worker is that she or he is always between things. The master of the art appreciates the muddle that is life and demands a profession that dances down a razor's edge. The worker who has "it" is the worker who knows that between me and thee is a fuzzy ball, a place where you invite "the other" to come in. To place hands upon the keys and make music. A place to cast off the cast iron of failed expectation and work in the muddle of the moment. What will emerge is anyone's guess, but at least it is not the pain of what once was.

If life were black and white, we'd have no need for social work. Police and lawyers and judges and accountants could solve most of what could be called conflict. But life is really quite a gray thing, and despite the anger that wells in those who rail against gray, who want things black and white, they know they need us.

No one wants to see a child endangered. And no one wants to see a family's privacy breeched. Yet, it is the privacy of the family that allows the craziness we need to stay sane in the public. But the craziness can go too far, and private matters become public concerns. We need nonjudgmental judges. We need those who can enter respectfully into the middle of our private muddles and echo the outside of our public rule. We need those who can understand the craziness that keeps us sane, and yet interpret the taboos that glue us together. We need advocates of the infinite diversities individuality provokes...and speak it to the Leviathan, and make it understand.

I'm always impressed with how many people don't know what social workers do; and therein lies our power. If others cannot define you,

you can define yourself. You can be the artist of your own practice with others. You can dwell inside the interstice, you can be in the place that is in between.

If you are young and you hear me now, in your future, hear this: the middle is not as dead as it appears. It is the fear of the hand that is not sure that it will strike the key correctly. It is the weary knowledge that work is hard, and yet the work will be done. It is the pain that will subside but not be lost, but will be carried. It is a glance that looks without, and within, in an instant. If you are old, and you hear me now, you will recognize your past and acknowledge the debt you owe to many you have learned from and celebrate the moments when you know that you were in the middle—you were "in the zone," and you had moved the world, in just the smallest way. In just a way that looked into you, and out of you. In just a way that a hand strikes a chord upon a piano. And in that note, nothing was ever the same.

I don't know how to end this, so I'll just stop in the....

Note: This story was originally published in 2007 in HUMAN BEHAV-IOR AND THE SOCIAL ENVIRONMENT, by Katherine van Wormer, New York: Oxford University Press.

In the E.R.

In early December, the air is gray and cold. What starts as a modest breeze off the harbor gets funneled by the faces of multi-story buildings on Monument Street, whipped into a biting blast that always seems to be in one's face. As I walk the blocks from the parking garage, I pass underneath the canyons of the Johns Hopkins Hospital. Towering above me stand many floors of surgery, therapy, and patients. Thousands of people bustle about in a brisk pace that insiders call "a Hopkins Walk." I am headed to the end of the block, the corner of Monument and Wolfe Streets. Of this huge medical complex, this is the basement. This is the Hopkins Emergency, and I'm the social worker on the 10 a.m to 7 p.m. shift.

There are five ambulance doors, and by this time in the morning, four of them are already filled with the orange and white "cracker boxes" of the BCFD (Baltimore City Fire Department). I walk toward the big electric street doors of the department, emblazoned with the logo of the lofty Hopkins "Dome," and the very clear words, "DO NOT PUSH." I smile inwardly as I think about how later tonight, I'll be giving 4th year meds a lecture on ethics and the emergency room. I will ask them to stand outside with me, read those words, and consider all the possible messages they imply.

The waiting room is packed, as usual. Despite all the efforts of bright paint on modern architecture, it still has the ambiance of a bus station. There are about 80 sullen, tired, and mostly black people, hunkered in coats and plastic chairs. Around them whiz physicians, residents, nurses, med students, and me, mostly white, and mostly looking like they are always in a hurry. I know that some of these people will be sitting here, still waiting, when my shift ends.

I throw my coat in a corner of the closet that is my office and see the notes that have piled waiting for me this morning.

A nurse has donated some clothes for a "clothes closet" I have set up for our homeless patients (who are not an uncommon population, but tend to be treated at times with less than a full measure of respect). I stack them according to blouses, shirts, pants. I secretly hope she will see these clothes walk out a few days from now on the frame of some now-nameless person. I hope it will decrease the distance between them.

Sleeping in the holding area is a young man with no apparent medical problem who says he is seventeen—a runaway from San Diego. I tell him I'm here to help. He has had breakfast, and I am arranging an early lunch while I try to offer him opportunities to tell his story. It is a detailed and confused tale, and the few bits of fact that emerge don't add up. I make some phone calls and find out that none of the addresses in San Diego exist. I go back and forth a few times, getting a new piece of information with each visit. Seeking some resources for possible referral, it seems this young man has already spent some time telling slightly different stories at both the city Department of Social Services and Traveler's Aid. Confronted with this information, and a continued offer of assistance, he indicates he's not really from San Diego, but is an undocumented alien from Jamaica. He asks for bus fare to the Consulate in Washington, D.C., forty miles away. I am incredulous, as the accent he has sounds pretty American to me. We have a nurse in the unit from Kingston, and I ask her to help me interview the young man. It becomes quickly apparent that he's lying again, and he gets angry. I tell him I figure he's probably in a pretty tight spot, and I'd like to help him....I don't need the whole truth, but he's gotta come close enough so that I can find his best way out of this emergency room. He stares at me angrily. Silent.

The klaxon goes off and a garbled radio voice says we have five minutes to two incoming medical emergencies via ambulance. I tell the angry fellow to enjoy lunch, and I'll be back in an hour. Before I even get back to my office, one of the cases is coming through the E.R. doors on its way to Critical Care Bay One. Shortly after, Bay Two is also filled with activity. I have flagged down the paramedics from both units to get what little I can on addresses, names, and any family who may have been present. I have donned gloves and go through the critical care rooms, picking up the cut-off clothes and searching for identifying materials. I find a purse in Bay 1, a wallet in Bay 2. The wallet in Bay 2 tells me a lot about a Mr. Tolliver. He's a barber, a mason, a husband, and he's been to this E.R. many times in the past three years with heart problems. There is a well worn photograph of him and a woman when they were both much younger and happier.

Through the elbows and tubes and paddles, I can look into both bays. I can see that both patients are elderly and unconscious. I set up the family rooms for relatives—quiet places where anxious, waiting people can be located. A small elderly woman and her adult daughter come looking for the patient in Bay 2. I inquire if she is Mrs. Tolliver. I offer the orientation and support that this crisis usually calls for. I prepare them for a "medical episode." The little woman's coat smells of mothballs and the faintest hint of stale cigar. They are quiet, trembling, and tragic.

The patient in Bay 1 recovers from the brink of death in 30 minutes, and is stable enough to be sent upstairs to a cardiac care unit. Bay 2 appears to be DOA and the resuscitation effort seems to go on forever. It is "early in the month"—a euphemism that means the E.R. is staffed with new residents and interns, and they need the practice trying to keep people alive. I guess it's better they practice on somebody who's pretty much dead than somebody who's pretty much alive. I am never easy with this decision.

After well over an hour, Weaver, the medical resident "calls it." I will help him break the news. I help a nurse with the quiet task of tidying up the body. Weaver is on the phone and smiling. His patient has died, but the blood gases and electrolytes induced during the resuscitation effort are the mimics of viability. "Harvard Lytes, man, we got Harvard Lytes!" Weaver says to me. I reach and touch his arm in the enthusiasm. "That's great, Martin," I say. "You are very good at what you do. Now, you need to take a moment, switch gears, and go with me to the family room to tell this patient's wife that her husband is dead." Weaver stiffens and I continue my hold on his elbow. My grasp has shifted from one of celebration to one of support. "Uh...yeah, yeah. Let's go do it. Uh, what was this guy's name?"

In the family room, Mr. Tolliver's survivors sit quietly. I have been in and out in the past hour and have kept them informed. They are prepared to hear that he has died, but until it is said, there is always a prayer upon hope. I have done this with Weaver before, many times. His style is to hem and haw, and when he's really uncomfortable, he starts to go into intricate detail and use medical jargon. He's getting better. Today, he skips the jargon and offers only a moderate amount of highlight about the rescue effort. I offer a brief clarification to the family that both prods him and allows for a moment to catch his mental breath. He enters back into the conversation simply: "I'm sorry, Mrs. Tolliver, we did everything we could, but your husband's heart just gave out. He's gone."

"Johnnie's dead?" she asks quietly.

"Yes ma'am," Weaver replies.

I ask the wife and daughter if they'd like to go back with me to the treatment room to see him and they numbly agree. I look over my shoulder and find that Weaver has gone. He has done his job with Bay 2. He goes back to work with the living. I will go with Mrs. Tolliver and her daughter to face their loss.

Back in Holding, the sullen young man looks a little less sullen, perhaps now a bit resigned. I figure he figures he's run out of time and stories. He's not been hassled by anybody in the last hour, and he got a meal, so maybe, just maybe, this worker will play it square with him. The story that emerges this time is vague enough in the details that it has more of the ring of truth to it. He's from Philadelphia, and has gotten into some trouble with "associates," to whom he sold some crack. He left Philly in a hurry. The car he stole broke down, and he was lucky to get it off I-95 and not attract attention from the Toll Authority police. He has a grandmother in D.C. and he's trying to get to her house. I tell him this one "sounds like it could just be a phone call away," if he gives me the grandmother's telephone number. He hedges for a bit, and then says that he burned her before, and he's not sure she will help. I tell him why don't we give it a try, it's just phone calls.

The klaxon goes off again and some disembodied dispatcher's voice reports that we have 12 minutes to prepare for a pediatric chopper incoming from the Eastern Shore. The peds nurses start preparing a bay. A resident calls up to peds-neuro to get a team on the way down to the E.R. Over the radio, a medic starts firing a report. On board is a little girl, apparently run over as somebody backed out of a driveway. One can hear the medic coming in over the static with numbers and facts about her condition that reveal she is strong, but hovering. There is attention in his voice. Somewhere over the Chesapeake Bay, he is focused on this bleeding child, and yet he knows it is just a matter of time and space before what was a situation on a driveway becomes a medical episode in the trauma center. All the people and scenery shift around except for the little girl in front of him.

Back in Holding, I am talking to the seventeen-year-old's grand-mother. At first she is angry that I am bothering her about this grand-son who has-no-respect-and-he-lies-and-he-cheats-and-he-steals. Then she catches her breath and she wants to know why he's in-the-hospital, and is-he-hurt and is-he-gonna-be-okay? I take a moment to reassure her about his present medical condition without elaborating on his po-tential social or legal status. I want to put them together on the phone. I ask if she can talk with him for a little bit, and she agrees. I cover the mouth piece as I hand him the phone. "Be nice to this old lady," I warn. "She cares more about you than anybody in Baltimore does."

The child from the Eastern Shore is now an unconscious case in Bay 3. Except for the thin red trickle from her right ear, and faint bruise above her right eye, she seems an otherwise unmarred 4-year-old. She is the center of an ever-expanding audience that is the hallmark of a pediatric critical care case. The room fills up with interns and residents and nurses from trauma teams that all own some piece of her recov-ery: Neuro, Internal Medicine, PICU, Surgery. The Peds trauma team is involved in all the work of initial assessment, and consults take place, being fired over shoulders. She is a well of attention, absorbing eyes and hands and thoughts about her vital signs.

Many of these people are "players," but many more are just "watch-ers." They have an "interest in the case," as a strategy develops to put this broken little girl back together. Those in the outermost rings crane their necks to see. They momentarily join into brief conversations with another spectator who is not central to the action. This is a teaching university hospital, and this is one of its pick-up classrooms. I watch a young surgical resident, who is backed into a far corner, and make a mental note about him. He is standing on a chair so that he can see. His hands are gloved and hold each other.

The beautiful child who looked "like a keeper," begins to "go sour," and what seemed mostly a head trauma goes into a full court surgical press. Before this is over, the floor will fill with blood and fluids, trash and terse words will fly freely, and a young woman will cut open and reach into the child's chest and squeeze her unmoving heart, hoping to make it move. When the collective hope is exhausted, someone in Attending's clothes says softly, firmly: "Thank you everyone. We're done here." There is a quiet embarrassment, and the once densely packed room becomes almost instantly empty. I turn to prepare a family room.

On my way back through the waiting room, I am flagged down by the sullen teenager, who is now not sullen, but smiling and waving and looks as if he has become my best friend. "Hey man! I'm outta here," he says. "My moms n' pops is on the way."

"You got a ride," I say.

"I got a ride." he smiles back.

"You be straight with that old lady," I wave my finger at him. "She loves you."

"Thanks, man," he says. "I owe you."

I ask him to tell me where he left the car he took from Philadelphia, and without a beat he gives me a corner about six blocks away. I shake his hand and walk back to the critical care bays.

Bay 3 has been cleaned, and is empty except for two figures. I look in from an adjoining room. Beneath the white-green hospital light, the dead child lies under stark white sheets; all the tubes and machines are gone. The young surgical resident I had noted earlier is the only person in attendance. He has bathed the little girl's face, and is trying to pack her leaking right ear with some nasal gauze. He is silent, and there are tears on his face. The packing will not stay put and keeps spilling out of the dead child's ear. He keeps trying to push it back in and keeps failing. He repeats this process over and over and seems stuck at the task. His hands have the slightest tremble. I move noiselessly up to the young resident and add a hand to his packing. In a moment, it is secure. I offer my hand, "It's Doctor Menedez, isn't it?" "Yes," he grips me back tightly, still fixed upon the little girl's face, "Reuben."

"Let's get some coffee, Reuben," I say, "I need a cup."

"Yeah. Thanks," he nods.

I am called a while later to the triage desk. A large, soft black man who is well known to me is standing across from the nurse. She has a slightly exasperated smile and she makes a motion of introduction with her hand. He has apple butter cheeks and a blank stare. He wears a racing cap.

"I don't feel so good. I don't feel so good—uh hum, uh hum," he quietly drones.

"I don't feel so good. I don't feel so good—uh hum."

"Turn off the machines. Turn off the machines—uh hum, uh hum."

"Turn off the machines. Turn off the machines—uh hum."

I know this man as Willy. I smile and offer my hand, which he takes limply. "Okay Willy, let's look around," I say, and we start to walk around the intermediate care unit. We peek in at the Asthma Room. We look into Holding. I make some reassuring observations about the environment around us, and nod at the people who pass by. People who know me and Willy make smiles and nod back. It becomes clear after five minutes that any machines of any concern are all turned off. Willy's shoulders relax and I walk him out onto the street. He will come back in two weeks after his Prolixin clinic appointment and we will do this inspection again.

Morrison, the sector "cage officer," has swung by, looking for this nurse he wants to date. He gives me a wink and says I must be Willy's best friend. I wink back at Morrison and tell him I'm everybody's best friend. We hang out together at the triage desk and shoot the breeze for a while. All the time, Morrison has an ear cocked to his radio.

The cage car officer patrols the entire Eastern District. He responds to sectors where officers have made an arrest, and transports the ar-rested person to the district lockup for booking. Morrison moonlights as a police officer in the E.R., and over time I have come to know him as a go-between for myself and some of the other sector officers. When issues of domestic abuse arise, the police and I have needs from each other, and Morrison has helped me make small breaks into the blue line. About every other month or so, I go on a "ride-along" for a shift with somebody in the district. I use the time to get tested by the officer at the wheel, and make some points about how we can help each other in those sticky situations. Afterwards, we will go to the Police Union Club and have too many beers. There have been some times now when I have been called from my office to go to some address in the neighborhood and help the officer on the scene. I feel good that these relationships are working.

"Hey Morrison," I punch lightly at his shoulder, "If you promise not to ask where I got it, I'll give you a present." Morrison thinks for a moment and then bites, "Okay, what?"

"There's a green Jeep Cherokee with Pennsylvania plates near the corner of Broadway and Eastern Avenue. It's outta gas and it might be hot from Philadelphia. I'm psychic."

"Cool," says Morrison, and he bends down to his radio.

After hours, the little girl's mother has arrived. As I escort her to the family room, she asks me if the child is all right. When I hesitate, and tell her that I am going to get Dr. Silvertson to come and talk to her, she knows her daughter is dead and she begins to wail and fling about, beating me on the chest. I wrap her with one arm, while waving off security guys with the other. We shuffle into the quiet of the family room to face some facts.

Sometime later, when she has composed herself and had a conversation with the physician in charge, we go into the quiet of Bay 3 and spend some time with the dead girl's body. The mother strokes the little girl's forehead. "She looks like an angel now," she says quietly, "in heaven." I nod and hold her other hand. She wants to know if I want to see some pictures of the little girl from her wallet. At this moment nothing is more important to me, and we share the photographs.

When we are done, I send the child's body off to the morgue, and I place the mother in the care of her people, who traveled hours away from this E.R., back to the rural place where they came from, knowing their lives are changed forever. I am starting to get tired, and I hope there are no more child deaths tonight. I then quash the thought with my own magical prohibition about such desires, as they tend to back-fire upon me. It's a struggle with magic, I always face, here in the E.R. I sit behind the only electric doors in this neighborhood that look con-stantly onto poverty, death, and tragedy. I am buoyed at times by the human strength that emerges. The humor, courage, and compassion that creeps into those spaces in-between. I am always tugged by my wishes and hopes, against the hard facts of life in East Baltimore. I find a constant struggle between wishes and reality. I go get another cup of coffee, and as I sit looking out onto the ambulance dock, I see this little homeless guy shuffle out of the hospital, wearing a shirt I stacked in the "clothes closet" this morning.

I laugh to myself as I see this bit of serendipity walking down the street. No matter the costs of tragedy, there are little moments of quiet heroics as well. The E.R. is a place of disorder, and the worker who works best is the one who can go with the flow. Sometimes hours of boredom are punctuated by minutes of terrific activity. One has to think fast on one's feet. Up in the rest of "the house," life has more order. Workers get to schedule appointments. Even in the intensive care units, where death is a common visitor, there is a greater sense of control. One is deeper in the hospital; one is on the hospital's turf. The E.R. is more like a beach, where the sea and the land meet, changing each other over and over. To do social work in the E.R. takes the heart and mind of a surfer; each new person off the street is another wave to meet well.

It is six o'clock, and the fourth year meds are in a pile at the triage desk, waiting for me. Soon, they will be starting their rotation in the E.R., and I get three hours in this week to talk ethics, the state of wel-fare, and social services in the emergency room. They are dressed in street clothes and these little white jackets that some call "clerk coats." Some have developed an officious defensiveness, while others just look lost and bewildered. I meet each one of them well, handing them a donut. I start off by making a joke that this is one of "two places that's open 24 hours a day and has cops: Dunkin' Donuts and the E.R." We laugh for a moment, and then get ready for a little conversation.

"To understand emergency medicine, you have to understand the street," I say, motioning for them to follow me onto the sidewalk outside, where we can look up and face the leviathan of the hospital. "Now...look at these doors and consider what they say: DO NOT PUSH...."

Note: This story is reproduced with permission from the book DAYS IN THE LIVES OF SOCIAL WORKERS, 4th Edition, 2012, Linda M. Grobman, editor, Harrisburg, PA: White Hat Communications.

Sweetening for Frankie

Frankie came in for the "spray."

Homeless, morbidly addicted to alcohol, he was well known to the E.R. for the seizures that would envelop him when he could not pan-handle enough change for wine and he would go into an involuntary detox. He'd start seizing in the street, get picked up by an ambulance, and wind up in the E.R. We would stabilize the seizure, have him lie on a gurney while a "yellow bag" dripped into him, and then kick him to the street with a 3-day supply of Dilantin.

He was a feral person. His face swollen from booze and beatings, matted hair in snaky dreads, thick clothing tattered in layers and lay-ers that never came off his body, he had an appearance that was more gorilla-like than human. He would slowly lope back to his cardboard box under the viaduct, or some other random abandoned squat that he might be able to discover when it got colder. He scavenged whatever nourishment he could from dumpsters behind bodegas, or he would hunch behind the few corner chicken shacks of the neighborhood, pit-eously putting his hand out for some scraps. He was rarely rewarded. He was mostly scorned and chased and beaten like some dog in an al-ley. He wasn't permitted in any of the shelters or soup kitchens, usually because of some past infraction of a rule about alcohol or some erratic impulsive altercation that included violence, but mostly it was because he stank to high heaven.

He'd be back in a week or so with the same presentation.

He'd passively resisted almost all our efforts at help. I was sure he sold the Dilantin as soon as he walked out the door, to buy wine. I would give him clean clothes and offer to have him shower, but he would simply add the new clothes to the uppermost layer of whatever shrouds he was wearing. He would take cigarettes and candy bars if offered. If you gave him a sandwich, he would carefully inspect what it was made of before eating it.

But today he came in on his own power, and at the triage desk, he told the nurse he wanted to see the "spray man." The nurse, completely not understanding, but seeing that Frankie was not seizing, called me (as obviously anything that was not a medical emergency must just be a social work concern).

As I talked with him, he smiled and said he wanted "the spray." He reminded me that on a winter's day about a year ago, I had sprayed him with some orange deodorizer that I had gotten from the morgue. I had given him enough bus tokens to ride the number 8 bus all the way out to the suburbs and back three times. It had kept him from freezing to death.

But it was a sunny and warm summer day. I told him I wasn't going to help ride the bus. "Naw, man, I don't needs da bus. I needs to eat. But Sister Lillian at The Daily Bread won't let me in 'cause she says I smell. If you sprays me, maybe she let me have a samich."

I looked at him. "Frankie. I'll help you get a shower and some fresh clean clothes. Howabout that?"

He looked back at me. "Naw man, dat's too much work. Just make me smell like an ornge."

"It's really not too much trouble for me Frankie. I can get you a nice hot shower."

"Mister. It's not too much work for you, but it's too much work for me. I jus wanna be an ornge and maybe get a samich."

"OK, sir. I hear you. Come on down to my office, and I'll turn you into an orange." I sprayed him up and down and around with the powerful deodorizer.

He smiled, lumbering out of my office. "Sister Lillian gonna think I'm sweet. I bet she gives me sumpthin' to eat."

From then on, Frankie would show up about every other week or so looking for me to spray him. I offered to give him a can, but he refused, indicating he'd just lose it. "You got the touch, man. Only you know how to make me an ornge the best."

"OK, Frankie," I said. "Turn around."

Dancing in the Midst (2005)

Prelude

In late night Orange County, California, I ran into a friend and colleague in a hotel lobby. "What will you write this year?" he asked. I shook my head and muttered, "I don't know. I'm empty." It had been a year of balancing my real responsibilities teaching young people social work with the sometimes less real responsibilities of my "consultant" life. I had put people on planes to Budapest. There had been multiple trips to D.C. On more than one occasion, there had been conversations with lieutenant colonels in the middle of the night in the middle of the desert. "I don't know," I said. "I guess it's the war."

"Write to me," he said.

Dear Marshall:

I've done some thinking about our brief conversation in the hotel lobby. I went back to some notes that I've made to myself over the years. There were a few that seemed to hold together—to illustrate some of the thoughts I've been thinking this year...

Note from an autumn in my freshman year, Albright College:

This afternoon, we all had to attend a convocation in the chapel. The Dean of the college was to give a lecture that apparently he gives every fall. Last night, the guys on my end of the hall were all bemoaning our mandatory attendance inside, on what was sure to be a lovely afternoon for football and beer. Curiously, the upperclassmen in their lounge were actually arguing about what the Dean said last year. "No, what McBride really means is..." I heard one say passionately.

I think the title of the talk was something like "Why We Are Here" or something like that. He was not easy to listen to, as his voice is sort of high and sharp. But I was impressed with some of the things he said. He started out by saying we are not here "to get jobs." "There are plenty of jobs, and each of you will have more than you probably want." He said we are here to learn how to ask ourselves "the big questions." What is a good citizen? What is a good person? What is to be valued?

What is to be sacrificed? There were more. He said we could not hope to answer these questions in four years at Albright. What we could do was learn how to learn, and find ways of caring for others and ourselves while we struggled. This point struck me: he said, "The mark of maturity is one's ability to engage ambiguity with grace." What the hell does he mean by that?

Notes from a bedside in a long term care facility:

My boss told me Sol Abrams, the neurologist, asked me to consult on this 60-year-old woman. She was unlike any other "parkie"[2] I'd seen. Apparently, for some time now, instead of her tremors increasing in frequency to the point she would just stiffen, her body twitched persistently and rhythmically in a gross and generalized fashion. She was maxed out on anything that Sol could give her to no avail. The tremors had picked up in amplitude in the last few weeks. She was burning thousands of calories a day and was birdlike, despite copious amounts of Ensure daily. Locked "on" in this horrible state, until very recently, however, she had been lucid and involved. She had been a high school English teacher and loved to read, a vocation that had been assisted with some interesting bedside tools and her determined force of will.

Apparently she had recently slipped into psychosis, and nothing seemed to help. The internist had ruled out every possible reason for delirium. My review of history, discussion with family, nursing, and exam of the patient were inconclusive. I thought possibly depression, but it was difficult to assess her mood. I was about to admit defeat, when, reviewing the chart again, it dawned on me that perhaps she wasn't sleeping, but nursing wasn't of any help. I came back late in the night to find her in full churn, wide awake, and crazy. I called my boss and gave him my theory. "Let's knock her out," he said. We did. She slept 12 hours straight with the twitching markedly calmed by barbiturates. When she awoke, her "park" came full back on, but she was lucid.

We had an engaging interview that explored the difficult state she was in. Her exhaustion. Her bouts with depression. Her rages against her body and her ambivalence of death. And yet, she had moments of humor. Near the end, we had a delightful chat about W. Somerset Maugham's *The Razor's Edge*,[3] a book we both apparently loved. She asked if I would visit her again, and I told her that I would be seeing her often, as we had not licked "the sleep problem" created by what she called "the willies."

Over the next few months, we visited off and on as I made my rounds—sometimes in the morning, sometimes late at night. We talked often of Larry Darrell, Maugham's young man in search of meaning after World War I, and of what it meant to be on a razor's edge. We laughed about a description of enlightenment coming with twitches and convulsions. All the while, her muscles seized rhythmically. All the while, her body burned away. She grew exhausted, and we would "knock her out." She would sleep and temporarily refresh. But there was only so much nepenthe we could do with barbiturate against her "willies." Near the end, she would slip in and out of exhausted delirium. The night before she died, we had a psychotic conversation. She recognized me as Larry Darrell. She laughed and said this: "There is no black. There is no white. There is no razor's edge. It's a wonderful gray and I'm dancing in the mist. It's a wonderful gray, and I'm dancing in the midst."

A note in the car on the way to NHQ:

A billboard on the way to work advertises a brand of cigarettes. An appealing woman dressed in jeans and a tight shirt is in a crouch position, facing me. Her legs spread wide, her right arm rests on her thigh and the smoke in her hand dangles casually in that space between knees. She smiles invitingly. Only three words inhabit this mural with her. In big bold letters: Kool No Doubt.

What utter advertising Shakespearean genius! There is no doubt you will have her if you have no doubt about smoking our product. Indeed, even behind all the noise of your confusing life, this is what you seek, even greater than sex is to be free of doubt! Smoke these buddy, have no doubt.

It's either right or left, up or down, black or white. You're either for us or against us.[4]

Notes from a professor's afternoon:

I've been thinking about McBride recently and his comment years ago about ambiguity. I often tell my students about how social workers are called upon to do the paradoxical, or the oxymoronic, depending on one's view. Between the extremes of the public and the private are the places where, despite how black and white some people would like to have it, is that crisis of the gray. Into that place we must carefully walk: "Disinterestedly Interested," "respectful noseybodys," "nonjudgmental judges." How queer that it is a single species, human, and yet its diversity ranges by billions of individuals. Upon what path, and at what cost, does one try to be helpful between the extremes of "universal truths" and "cultural relativity"? No matter what we do, in someone's eyes we will be wrong, especially in a time now when so many are trying to speak in the language on "no doubt." There is error in every action of social work, and yet absolute need. Absolute art. These are the "big questions" of a social worker's life. How does one deal?

With some effort, and the help of the archivist at Simpson College in Iowa, I found that Robert McBride went on to become their 19th president and was well regarded. They named an annual lecture in his honor, and a baseball field. She said he was alive and well, and she gave me his home phone number. I called his home this afternoon. His wife answered and called him to the phone. I could feel frail gentility hanging in the sunlight of an Iowa living room, as we talked. He was gracious as I tested his memory with talk about a lecture he had given 30 years ago. He asked me what I did and how was I doing, and, in all, it was a much longer conversation than I had planned. It was pleasant and mutually respectful. As we came near the pleasantries of conclusion, I shared with him how impressed I had been with his prescience. I indeed have had many jobs...more than I needed at times. I have continued to struggle with all of the big questions, and have passed them along to others. "But how," I asked, does one "engage ambiguity with grace?" "Oh," he said, "I think you'll know how."

Postlude

Dear Marshall: I'm not sure if I'll write an essay to this list this year. But the more I thought about it, the more I realized I'm not empty after all. It's just that I've been so busy. So busy dancing in the midst.

Your buddy,
Ogden Rogers

Detoxing Wealth

He had just returned to the hospital on his own accord. The Friday before, he had escaped after dinner. He took a cab to the airport, and his private jet to Aruba. He apparently got high for a couple of days, hung out with some friends, and then decided to come back.

I asked why he had split. He looked me straight in the eye. "I needed a break from all this middle class culture. I know I need to get sober, but man, seriously, I gotta find a sobriety that wears a better class of threads."

Occupational Therapy Tool Number 7

His name was Frank, and his reason for being on the GeroPsychiatric Unit was a diagnostic work up for Alzheimer's disease. In recent years, he had become more forgetful and confused and had increasingly poor control of agitated outbursts.

Like many folks who came to the unit, he had a confused medical history of multiple medical diagnoses: diabetes, hypertension, congestive obstructive pulmonary disease. He had been going to multiple doctors and was on multiple medications. Like many folks who came to the unit, he lived alone and had few social supports. Like many folks on the unit, he had to deal with being in the strangeness of the hospital, not really wanting to be there, and having little to do with the hanging time between X-rays, cat scans, laboratory studies, psych testing, and interviews from people like me.

Consequently, he was wandering about the floor, asking people frustrating questions, and getting into irritable outbursts. As he was assigned to my practice, the nurses were getting concerned about his potential for violence and had asked me for an assessment for tranquilizing medication.

In the course of doing the history, I learned that Frank had been a custodian at an elementary school for the last 15 years of his work life. I asked him what that was like, and he said he enjoyed the frequent interchanges with children and teachers, got frustrated with toilets clogging up, but mostly he enjoyed the quiet of the hallways when children were in their classrooms and he would, as he said it, "push my broom."

Carmela was the housekeeper on the GeroPsych floor. I always maintained a courteous and friendly relationship with her. Always saying good morning, sharing the occasional coffee in the break room, mock-flirting in the hallway.... We had a running gag about winning the lotto and flying off to Cozumel.

I asked her if I could borrow a push broom so that Frank could mop the hall. She smiled, "For you, Doctor Rogers, anytheen."

After a brief orientation to the requirements and boundaries of the ward, Frank was off to his assignment, dressed in the hospital issue bathrobe and slippers. I went off to see other patients, but kept track of him in the corner of my eye. He pushed the broom with a smooth and practiced cadence, and after a few minutes, he hummed an old hymn softly. He worked one side of the hallway slowly for about twenty minutes, and then worked the other side. His third stroke took him down the middle. He spent about an hour sweeping the hall and then sat down for a spell in his room. He came out ten minutes later wearing an old baseball cap and proceeded to begin to push the broom again. He swept the floor about five times before lunch. In all of that time, he stayed to the task. He would smile a small smile and his attention to the nursing staff was reduced to just small cordial "good mornings" as he went up and down the hallway.

After lunch, he went back to his sweeping. This time he had cinched a belt around his bathrobe. Still humming to himself, he had found a pleasant old groove. The head nurse had observed my little intervention and approved, patting me on the head while I was doing some charting. "Clever little man you are, Doctor Rogers. I wonder how long this peace will last?"

I had no idea it would be so short. But not because of the patient. An hour later, a bearish man wearing a gray suit jacket and a frustrated demeanor sputtered at me while I was in the break room. Mr. Baccardi was the Housekeeping Department Head.

"Are you the person who gave that patient a broom?!" he demanded. I agreed and began to tell him the story of Frank, his Alzheimer's, and his history as a custodian.

"I don't give a damn how much experience he has," the Head of Housekeeping cut me off. "It's against hospital policy to let housekeeping equipment be used by anybody except housekeeping." He pulled up a black plastic 3-ring binder and pointed the rule out to me clearly.

No amount of persuasion by either me or the head nurse would change his mind. I tried as best as I could to explore the rule. Was it a safety issue? Was it a union thing? Wasn't there any way we could bend it? It was so clear that Frank's aimless wandering had found aim once put to the task of the push-broom. In the absence of the activity, I was sure that he would return to the more unstructured place that had been the wellspring environment increasing his anxiety and impulsive, possibly violent behavior.

Later that same day, I had to look in on another patient who was in the Physical Therapy/Occupational Therapy department. My patient was being seen by a PT to assist with her walking after breaking a hip in an auto accident. While I was there, I noticed a fellow seated at a table pouring metal nuts out onto a table, and then sweeping up the nuts with a small hand whiskbroom into a dustpan. He would pour the nuts out of the dustpan into a box, and begin the whole process over again.

Margie, the Director of Occupational Therapy, sat in the corner observing the man with the hand brush and dustpan, taking notes. I walked up to her discreetly. "Uh, Margie, what's that guy doing over there?" I asked. She explained that the patient was engaged in an exercise to help build his upper body strength and coordination.

"Yeah," I acknowledged, "but what's he doing it with?"

"A little hand whiskbroom and a dustpan." She looked at me incredulously.

"How do you keep from losing those things to housekeeping?" I asked.

"Oh," she replied, "they're not housekeeping. They're occupational therapy tools. See?" She went over to another dustpan on another table and flipped it over. In bright red nail polish on the back of the dustpan were the words: "OT Dept. #3."

"Margie," I muttered, lights firing off in the back of my head. "Do you have policies and procedures that cover these tools?"

"Oh, sure," she spat back. "They're inventoried. And have to be used as part of a prescribed OT treatment plan. See?" She pulled out a fat binder with color-coded tabs, and sure enough, there were all sorts of rules and regulations about that dustpan. I smiled. Margie was a good colleague of mine. She had been amenable to providing OT services on the floors for some patients who couldn't make it up to the department. I told here about my problem with Frank and the house-keeping supervisor.

I went to see Carmela and told her about Frank and her supervisor. She had seen the altercation earlier and formed even more personal opinions about her boss. I wondered aloud if somehow a broom that perhaps wasn't under careful supervision somewhere might get itself lost in the hospital and nobody would ever know it was missing. Carmela smiled at me. "For you, Doctor Rogers, anytheen.'"

A quick trip back up to OT. A few strokes of red paint, a spiral of red tape along a long handle for good measure, and a few new lines inserted into the OT Policy and Procedures handbook, and Frank was back to push-brooming the hallway. His posture was erect, his strokes light and deft. He was humming a hymn.

The next morning, after breakfast trays, I was doing some charts in the nursing station. My patient, Frank, cap and belt and push-broom, had showered for the day and had begun his studied efforts at dust in the hallway. It was quiet and peaceful.

On unseen cue, Mr. Baccardi arrived on the hall doing his rounds. He saw Frank, and sputtered. He marched into the nursing station and looked down at me. "I told you yesterday we can't have patients using housekeeping equipment. What seems to be the problem here, Dr. Rogers?" He glowered.

I looked up from my writing and over the nursing station to the patient in the ball-cap. "Frank," I called out, "come over here." Mr. Baccardi stiffened. I reached out for the push-broom. "We don't have a problem, Mr. Baccardi," I noted, handing the brightly festooned janitorial tool to him. "See right there. Painted in red. That's not housekeeping equipment. That's Occupational Therapy tool number 7. I won't ever let a patient use housekeeping equipment again. I promise."

Mr. Baccardi turned and walked away. I looked down the hall. Carmela smiled. The nurses smiled. I smiled. Frank hummed a little and pushed his broom.

Day-At-a-Glance (age 30)

Friday

0600. Up and get the coffee going. Number One Son needs to get up and be changed. Start breakfast with him in highchair in the kitchen. Listen out of one ear to the TV news. Carol up and getting ready for the day. Have second cup of coffee while looking at various parts of the newspaper's front section while the boy eats Cheerios.

0700. Listen to NPR while commuting to first hospital of the day.

0745. Read inpatient charts while nurses are doing their a.m. cares and patients are breakfasting. Call in referrals for patients that need specialists.

0800. Start rounds. 7 patients on the Geropsych ward this morning. See each one for about a half hour. Essentially a mental status exam if they are compromised, severely demented, depressed, or psychotic. Supportive psychotherapy, addressing issues if they are functioning at higher levels. Read charts and consult with medical PA as to labs and tests coming back or consults to order. Monitor referral and treatment to OT, PT, and group TX as needed.

1000. Discuss medical status of patients shared with internal medicine with the Medical Physician's Assistant.

1030. Discuss patients over the phone with supervising psychiatrist. Make recommendations, write orders per his instructions.

1100. Walk over to psych unit to see patient admitted yesterday from the E.R. 16-year-old admitted "freaking out" with facial symptoms of dyskinesias and neuroleptic Parkinsonism. All of the neurologic symptoms have abated. Take history. Long story, short: inexperienced drug taking...bought pills from another high school friend who told her they would make her high...my guess based upon her description is she bought some Haldol. Will probably release tomorrow after we meet together with her mom and make an outpatient plan.

1200. Eat lunch in car. Drive across town to Jefferson Village Medical Center. Have 4 patients scheduled.

1230. Marlys: 43-y.o. single woman who spent the first 40 years of her life in some form of institutionalized care. First 20 years in "school for the retarded" (she wasn't). Second twenty years in "State Hospital for the Insane" (also, not really, just not ready for the world after the first 20 years). Seen supportively 30 minutes each week. Lives in group home. Working ever so slowly on goal of independent living. Today: we talk about a man she met in day treatment program that she would like to be her boyfriend.

1300. Daniel: 52-y.o. divorced engineer with depression. Depressed after divorce. Divorce finalized three years ago. Still grieving. Still depressed. Seen weekly for last two years. He spends much of the session harping about being treated unfairly at work.

1400. Mitch: 38-y.o. professional baseball player for a major league team. Also divorced. Drinks too much. Parties too much. Sleeps around too much. His bat, once in the upper 200s, has now slumped to lower 200s. Started playing ball right out of high school and has never thought about doing anything else. The front office has started to threaten him with a trade down to the minors if his game doesn't pick up. I'm impressed how young a mid-life crisis comes to a sports pro.

1500. Clarence: 62-y.o. depressed fellow with some early dementia symptoms and a long history of alcohol abuse and lives alone. Abstinent now for years, but never one to join the "recovery movement." Session spent supportively, we're slowly working on getting him to socialize more at the local senior center.

1530. Drive uptown to second hospital of the day.

1600. Consult: 26-y.o. male with newly diagnosed Multiple Sclerosis. Complaint of depression and mild suicidal ideation. Feeling of crisis as new diagnosis is overwhelming him. Worried about what this will mean for his entire future. We discuss the extent of his suicidal thinking. He agrees to a "self-safety plan" and an outpatient visit in my office in two days. Write it up.

1700. Consult: 73-y.o female from a major city long-term center admitted for acute confusional state, initially to internal medicine service as there was some cardiac instability on presentation. Cardiac status now clear. Confusion persists. Still impulsive and dysphoric. Internist wants to know if we can help her over at GeroPsych. He's worried if he sends her back to nursing home she'll "bounce" back in just a couple days. Transfer and admission to Geropsych will buy her another 5 to 10 days of inpatient care time to see if we can figure out what's going on, and can we either reverse behavior or devise a plan for management. Call patient's family, discuss admission. Call my supervising psychiatrist, discuss admission. Everybody agrees. Call Nursing to arrange transfer and admission to GeroPsych. Do the paperwork.

1830. Drive across town to our "private" offices. Scarf a hamburger along the way.

1900. Private patient. Joseph: a 36-y.o. paramedic and his wife for couples counseling. There are significant tensions in their relationship, most of which are getting better by helping them to establish boundaries and rules for "fair fighting." They have been smiling more and fighting less. I think soon we'll begin discussing ending treatment.

2000. Do a half hour of paperwork. Dictate some notes. Write up some care plans for insurance companies.

2030. Drive home. See family. Talk with Carol about problem with the refrigerator. I guess we'll have to buy a new one. Watch some cop show on TV but not really follow story as I'm thinking about a problem I'm having with my dissertation.

2200. Brush teeth. Go to bed.

2330. Wake up halfway through a dream. I am lost in a rainforest in the middle of a monsoon. I am trying to start a fire but all the tinder and kindling is wet and the rain is coming down in torrents. Suddenly, a gentle breeze comes from behind me and parts the foliage, showing me the way out of the forest. I wake up with a feeling that I should remember this dream, but I don't know why.

Halfway Down the Red Line

I got on the Metro at Shady Grove around nine-thirty in the morning, a 45-minute ride on the Red Line to the airport and out of Washington, D.C. The car was empty, and I sat near the door facing backward.

At Rockville, a young black woman got on, sitting also near the door and facing forward. Two white men got on and sat across from the woman, each sprawled in a different seat. One was older, in his thirties, barrel chested and short with well-muscled arms and close cropped hair. He was in conversation with his companion, a tall, soft, and pudgy young man with longish hair and thick glasses...I guessed perhaps 18.

He was loud, the short man, and in the emptiness of the subway car, he seemed even louder, yet apparently oblivious to the other two passengers in the car. He was talking to the youth about some article in his newspaper, apparently about some story about affirmative action. In very short order, his conversation became instructional, a lecture. He was telling the youth what an evil this idea was, and how it gave advantages to "HO-MO-SEX-uals" and "NE-groes." The white man, he went on in different iterations, didn't have a chance.

The soft youth just nodded. Occasionally, he muttered a "yeah" or asked a small question. The older man continued his narrative, a mixture of racist remarks and a basic plot of persecution by other races against Caucasians. Down through the stops across the Maryland suburbs, he continued racial slurs and paranoid quips in a voice that carried well to the young woman and myself. I marveled at his oblivion of we, the other passengers in the car, as he continued his monologue to his protégée.

I looked up at the young woman. She wore the uniform of someone who cleaned in a hotel or waited in a diner. She looked tired and resigned. Her eyes were closed as if she was resting. If she opened them at all, she looked straight ahead, blankly, and through me.

I looked at myself, a reflection in the Plexiglass near the subway car door. Was I so small and white and older that I had become invisible? How could this obnoxious bantam spout this angry noise as if both of us were not here? How was it that I had sat silently listening to this vitriol without muttering a word?

The train approached the Woodley Park station, and the two men approached the door. I guessed they were going to the zoo. The train-man announced the station and indicated which doors would soon open. I smiled at the older fellow and said, "Brother, what's great about this democracy is your right to instruct that young fellow in your truth."

"Amen to that, man," he responded, smiling back. The train slowed to almost the stop. The mechanical women's voice of the Washington Metro announced, "Doors Opening!"

"Ya know what's also great about this democracy?" The doors opened.

"What?" asked the loudmouth, still smiling, stepping toward the platform.

I lost my smile. "My vote cancels out yours," I said.

The black woman leaned forward and pointed to the youth. "And mine cancels out his!"

The car doors closed and the train sped on. The woman and I looked at each other, silent again, each of us shaking our heads in disbelief.

The trainman announced the next station. "Dupont Circle. Doors open on the right."

It's a Black and White Thing

Jim and I got along famously. We took doctoral classes together in the school of social work. We both had young families. Jim had invited me for a visiting professorship at the BSW program where he worked. I enjoyed trading barbs with him as he had the office right next to mine. We both enjoyed talking about social work and the events of the day. We saw the world through many of the same glasses.

Which is why I was so surprised when the day came that we disagreed.

One day I was reading an article in the student newspaper. The item that became our dispute was about African American students organizing to have an all-black student dorm. I had casually mentioned the article over lunch and said that I thought it was a bad idea. Jim looked up from his soup and said he disagreed. It was a good idea, he said. Black students should have their own dorm. I should indicate that I am a Caucasian and Jim is African American.

We began to argue our positions, but the lunch time was running out and we both had classes to teach. We agreed, however, to meet again for lunch and hash the disagreement out.

For the next day at lunch, Jim and I, who agreed on so much, focused on the arguments that led to our difference.

"It's hard to be black on this campus. There are so many white people. To be black on this campus is to go to class surrounded by white people, go to meals surrounded by white people. Be in discussions with lots of white people. It's a comfort to be able to be around one's own folk. To have a place at the end of the day you can just be around black people and not have to feel that you have to be prepared to explain blackness. One can just enjoy being in a small world of African Americans."

"I'm hearing you and understand," I said. "I understand taking comfort from being with one's folk. But, here's my point: Integration in housing is the law of the land. It wasn't always so. Discrimination was the law. Segregation was the law. If we allow people to discriminate for 'good' reasons, what prevents people from discriminating for 'bad' reasons? If we are going to have a rule of law, it should apply equally and fairly to all."

"I think," said Jim, "I understand where our fundamental differences lie."

"Where?"

"You, I suspect, trust law as a concept serving fairly as a social mediator of relations between people."

"And you?" I asked.

"While I want that to be true, in my lifetime I've seen law and its enforcement as a vehicle of unfairness and oppression. I don't trust law the same way that you do. I suspect you think you can solve problems with law, and I often see law as the problem."

I thought about this for a while. "So, if we allow black students to segregate on their own accord, should we allow white students to be able to do the same thing?"

"No, if black students want to live with white students, they should be allowed to."

"But white students could be refused if they wanted to live in a black dorm?"

"Yes. The minority should have a right to its own enclave."

"Why?"

"Because they are a minority in a larger white world. It's harder on them."

"OK....I understand holding people more important than law. But, when will we ever know when the law can be a fair and equal thing? When will we reach the balance point between this racial divide?"

Jim thought for a while. "That's a really good question. I don't have a good answer for you. I would hope in my children's lifetimes we can reach that point. I don't know if I will know it in my life."

"I like eating lunch with you, Jim. It's never boring."

"Yeah, same," said Jim. He smiled. "You're OK for a white guy."

Paging Jesus

My first assessment of the morning.

The nurses said that she was increasingly despondent, delusional, and hallucinating. Her internist said her sugars were getting better and he wanted to discharge her soon, but she seemed outrageously depressed. Her daughter was angry that somehow being in the hospital was making her mother crazy, and she was totally unconvinced she wasn't being made sick by some medication.

The 77-year-old moderately obese lady with a history of diabetes, hypertension, and some mild peripheral vascular disorder, in the unit for three days, had been physically getting better, but was emotionally distraught and depressed.

I'm always sensitive to the possibility of delirium, but in reviewing her chart, I couldn't find anything that stood out. She had no prior psychiatric history. Perhaps just the stress of patienthood was making for a psychotic break.

"God is calling for me, but he can't hear me. I must be slipping toward hell." She sobbed, and I held her hand. Everything about her was cognitively intact, and indeed, except for the last 72 hours, she had no significant indications for depression. The onset was very acute. I searched my thought for crisis intervention possibilities. I asked if she had sought or received spiritual comfort. She did, and had. Her priest had come by, but she was still quite upset.

"Tell me about what is happening with God," I asked.

"He keeps calling me," she said. "He is looking for me, and I call back, but he can't hear me. God is looking for me, but he can't find me. Every night, he's been looking for me in this hospital, but he can't find me. I know I've sinned, but I don't want to go to hell." She cried. Deep heaving sobs. Disconsolate.

"When he calls you, what does it sound like? Do you hear it in your head?" I asked, seeking to understand the quality of her experience.

"Oh, he has the sweetest softest voice." She relaxed a moment. "This is The Lord," she said. "He keeps seeking me, but cannot hear my reply. Do you think I'm crazy?"

I met her question directly. "I think you're very upset, and understandably so. I'm sorry you feel so lost right now, and I'd like to try and help. Can I come back and visit you later today?" She agreed, and I left.

My supervising psychiatrist and I had our usual morning call, discussing the hospital workload and the various patients and their status. I told him I didn't quite know what to think about the lady hearing God. She could be depressed, we agreed, but I was not sure she was psychotic. I wanted more time to assess her situation.

I stopped by and looked in on the woman one more time. I had spent the evening in a nearby office seeing some outpatients and had stopped in the hospital late on my way home. The night shift had come, and the nurses were all in report. I looked in and saw the patient was asleep and the lights had been dimmed, since the visiting hours had ended. I started reading her chart.

I knew the night shift nurse, who had once been the girlfriend of an old roommate of mine. We talked old times for a while. She was seeing another guy now, a homicide detective with the city police. We talked about our old times together at the SEPpH. I asked her about the patient, and she said that she'd had a few outbursts on night shift, almost without warning, and bolted out of sleep.

As I sat at the nurses' station, I became aware of an occasional overhead page I heard, almost whispered, by the hospital operator: "Mrs. Lord, 3313...Mrs. Lord, 3313." Several times in the next hour, I heard a similar page.

"Who's Mrs. Lord?" I asked the night nurse.

"She's the 11-7 supervisor," she answered. "Why?"

I smiled. "She's brought me closer to Jesus."

Mistaken Identity

I was writing on some patient charts behind the nurses' station when I saw him walk by. He was wearing the mid-length lab coat of the first-year resident, but I recognized him as the wild boy I used to party with years ago in undergraduate school. He'd gone on to do laboratory science, but recently must have finished medical school.

I bolted up from my chair, dressed in shirtsleeves, and sprang into the hall. I called out behind him, "Art! Hey Artie! Yo, Art Crooms!" I started down the hall with my hand outstretched.

The resident wheeled around and recognized me. A shadow fell across his face informed by a past he'd rather forget. Here was someone who had seen him do bong hits. Here was someone who knew he used to body surf the stairs at the TKE house. He took a step toward me and shook my hand. He pulled me closer and spoke in almost a whisper.

"Hey. Hi, Og. Look. It's been years. Hey, look. I'm Dr. Crooms now, not Art or Artie. It's Doctor Crooms. Got it?"

There was a tiny, angry piece of me that wanted to pull out my business card, point out my Ph.D., and discuss my relationship with the practice that was the psychiatric attending in the hospital where he had just joined as medical resident. There was a piece of me that wanted to transport him back to a locker room somewhere in the past of college life, and snap a wet towel at him. But the angels of my better nature took control. I shook his hand back.

"Welcome to medical residency, Dr. Crooms. I'll be seein' you around the halls."

He smiled back weakly and took off, clearly consumed with way too many thoughts to understand just now.

I went back to my charts. I shook my head and smiled.

The Principle of Self-Determination[5]

I got the invitation from Bob. He was inviting me to a celebration on a Sunday afternoon. He was a most thoroughly disagreeable man, and I was sure the original plan would fall apart and he'd wind up back in the nursing home. I told my wife I didn't think I'd be long, probably "just we three and tea." But, I get ahead of my story.

The client was a 56-year-old Caucasian male who was paralyzed from the waist down after an auto accident. His life had been slowly falling apart for years before the accident. He was a teacher with a master's degree by profession and kept getting fired for his inappropriate behavior. By the time of the accident, he was essentially homeless. The accident put a roof over his head in a nursing home, a large long-term care facility in the urban center.

He came to my attention by referral from the hospitalist. He had been admitted briefly to the hospital in which I practiced for some urinary tract infection, and was about to be transferred back to his long-term care center. The hospitalist said the patient complained of depression.

He was very personality disordered. Grandiose, angry, projective, foul-mouthed, and at core, a bigoted fellow who was prejudiced against just about every racial, ethnic, religious, and sexual identity. The problem was, he was surrounded by people different from himself who were his caregivers, and he regularly and impulsively mouthed off his personal disapproval with everyone he met. He said he was depressed because he was going back to the nursing home and he hated it there. He quickly agreed to see me for a weekly visit at an outpatient office I had about six blocks away. He didn't think I could be of any help, but "if nothing else, it will get me out of that hell for a few hours."

I really didn't like him.

So the plan emerged over the first few weeks that if he could get out of the nursing home and live somewhere else, he'd be less depressed. The problem was finding a place to live that could support his substantial physical needs. Group homes for the mentally ill could not support a guy in a wheelchair who needed regular bowel and bladder care. Group homes for the physically disabled did not want someone with so intractable a personality problem.

In the interim, we were able to get him "a change of scenery" twice a week as he started working on a second master's degree at the university near the nursing home. At Physical Therapy in the nursing home, he was working on the essential needed skill of independent living: being able to self-transfer from bed to wheelchair, and wheelchair to bed. He still did his best to piss off just about every human being at the nursing home as often as possible.

There was also the matter of funding. He had only a small Social Security Disability income, and all of his care was paid through Medicaid. In some ways, he was indeed too independent for nursing home care, but not independent enough for assisted independent living. We were going to have to work some new regulations from Medicaid to be able to pay for enough care from the Visiting Nurses Association. We were going to have to find some way of paying for affordable rent, in a barrier-free environment, and oh, there was the matter of tuition and books, and oh yes, I forgot, he was a pretty disagreeable man to be around.

It took about a year. On his part, this involved training on the skills of self-transfer, follow-through with various appointments with various persons or agencies that we were appealing to for resources, or changes of law or regulation. On my part, there was the exploration of finding those persons or agencies, advocacy for his situation, and weeding out the blind alleys or barriers from the potential collaterals who could help with his problem. All the while, there was the constant work on his various paranoid, aggressive, hostile, delusional, bigoted behaviors.

We slowly but surely put together a plan. The university where he was enrolled as a student owned an apartment complex, which was barrier free, close to his classes and other community amenities. The state (it took going all the way to an Assistant Secretary of Health) recognized the difficult situation and granted key changes in Medicaid funding required for his several needs. The home health agencies and a local clinic cooperated around the provision of his medical care, and they located "Angel."

Ah, Angel! The solution and nightmare that was the keystone of the whole plan. Angel (pronounced Ang-hell) was this meek, wonderful soul who was willing to take on much of the twice daily nursing and home health care that Bob needed for independent living. He was willing to do this for the low pay he was going to get from Medicaid, the split hours it would make in his day, and despite the verbal abuse that would be rendered by Bob. Angel was a Hispanic, Afro-Caribbean, gay man who was a certified nursing assistant working on his LPN.

The first few meetings of the two men were quite tense. I had spent some time with Angel preparing him for the client's personality, but I don't know how anybody could be prepared for the sort of abuse Bob could pour out. I think high intelligence makes nasty people even nastier. To his credit, Angel could filter out much of the insult and focus on the concrete needs of his future patient. To his credit, Bob could demonstrate that he could reign himself in on his abusive tendencies and come to recognize the importance of Angel to his overall goal of getting out of the nursing home.

Personally, I didn't think it would all last a month. He said he didn't think he would need to continue in outpatient treatment.

So, a year later, dressed in jeans and with low expectations, I found the social room of the apartment hotel where Bob lived. Inside were about 30 people sipping coffee or mimosas, dressed in power suits or Sunday finery: the CNO of the Visiting Nurses Association, the President of the University, two Assistant Secretaries of Health, several heads of home health care agencies, a couple of reporters, some professors, some neighbors, and Angel was working as a waiter. Bob called me his "guest of honor" and gave me a little plaque of recognition. There was a polite round of applause. I gave it all back by calling Bob a wonderful person to work with and a "fierce example of the spirit of human independence." The applause was much louder.

Privately, in small groups and out of earshot, everyone in the room confided in me that he was a most disagreeable man, but they admired his determination.

Everybody's Gotta Boss

For absolutely no particularly good reason I can remember, I was browsing through the *Federal Register*. I must have been in the library, killing time between classes, and I must have been waiting for some other reason, and it must just have been out on a desk or something, because, trust me, it is not the kind of reading one just picks up for fun.

Anyway, as I was flipping through it, I came across a change in the Medicaid regulations that expanded client eligibility onto the program. The rules expansion fit a client of mine, who had lost her Medicaid three years earlier, and her life had been made quite difficult as a result.

I double checked the text of the changes, carefully ascertained that what I saw was what I read, and in doing so, noticed that the changes had actually gone into effect a full year earlier. States had six months from date of publication to implement them.

The next day, I called my client and asked her if she could stop by my office. When she arrived, I told her I'd read some new information that might make her eligible again for a Medical Assistance card. I asked her some questions about her illness, her income, and housing status, and, confirming what I knew, I thought she might indeed be eligible. She was excited, and agreed to go down to the Department of Social Services the next day to see if she could apply.

The next day before lunch, I got a phone call from my client. She was upset and indicated that the DSS worker (who knew her well) told her she couldn't reapply, as she didn't qualify. The worker had actually processed her discontinuance paperwork two years earlier. I asked her if I could call her worker, and she enthusiastically agreed. After repeated calls all afternoon, and hours of waiting, I finally got the eligibility worker, who was reasonably exasperated with me.

"She don't qualify. You shouldn't of sent her down here and get her hopes all up. She's a mess on a good day."

I persisted. "Ms. Johnson, I hear you and I'm sorry she got all upset. But I read about a rule change that I think makes her eligible again."

"Don't know nothin' about it. Don't be sendin' her down here."

I asked to speak with Ms. Johnson's supervisor. Mr. Stanley, who I got after two lost transfers, one hang up, and also a good hour's wait, was equally unhelpful.

"I don't know what you are talking about. I have received no information about rules changes." I asked Mr. Stanley who he reported to, and he gave me the number of an assistant director who I could call in the morning.

Next morning, I started the telephone work with the assistant director. I didn't have to wait very long, as I was her first call of the day, but she couldn't help me as that kind of information came from a regional director. She didn't know anything about the *Federal Register*. She transferred me to the regional director, who put me on hold, and then my call got dropped. I called back and about an hour later, I got the regional director, a Mr. Holden, who gave me essentially the same answer the assistant director had given me. He also didn't care about the *Federal Register*. I asked him who was his supervisor.

"I don't have a supervisor. I'm a regional director," he informed me.

"I'm sorry. I misspoke," I said. "Who do you report to? I'd like to take my inquiry to a higher authority."

"I'm the authority," he said.

"I understand that, sir, but I think a mistake is happening. I need to speak to someone above you who is responsive to the federal government concerning Medical Assistance regulations."

"Well," he said. "That would be the Deputy Secretary of the State Department of Health, and he is outside the line of the application appeal process."

"Thank you. I understand. I don't want to make an eligibility denial appeal. I just want to talk to the Deputy Secretary." He gave me the office number.

The next day, after speaking to the Deputy Secretary's secretary, and calling back after he was in a meeting, and being on hold, I finally got the Deputy Secretary. He was a nice enough man but after a few comments, he cut me off and said it sounded like my client didn't qualify. I asked him about the changes in the federal regulations.

"What changes?" he asked. I was ready. I quoted him the 42 CFR Part 433, *Federal Register,* volume, number, date, and page number.

"How do you know about that?" he asked.

"What?" I asked. I took a breath, but then even in my tone, I began, "I read it in the library, just like anybody can. Now, can you help my client or not? I've been calling people for almost three days now, and the way I see it, the State of (name redacted to protect the guilty) is out of compliance with the law for over six months now. I have to make another call, and I don't know if it's to the State Attorney General, the Inspector General of the Department of Health and Human Services, or to the government editor of the biggest newspaper in the state."

There was a long silence on the phone. "Hold on, Mr. Rogers. Give me a minute."

I waited and listened to the holding music, which sounded like an old Doobie Brothers song. I waited through that song and was halfway through the next one, when the Deputy Secretary came back on.

"I want to thank you for bringing this matter to our attention. It appears some oversight has occurred and we will be devising some changes in our eligibility policy in the future."

"What about my client?" I asked.

"Tell your client to go to her District DSS office in the morning. My assistant will prepare that office to take a new eligibility application for her.

I thanked the Deputy Secretary for his time and attention. He thanked me. I thanked him again. My client got her new Medical Assistance card in 14 days. Everybody has a boss.

Mid-Life Crisis

In the mirror of my office bathroom, I was shaving. I had a date later that evening and I wanted to be as smooth as possible. The date was with a woman I had not seen in a couple of years. We had a story in the past and I was wondering if this would lead to a new chapter.

I had just seen my last patient of the week that afternoon. A woman named Cheryl Moon. A round woman in her middle 40s and with a diagnosis of severe borderline personality disorder. She had a chaotic 20-year history in and out of long-term psychiatric hospitalization. I had met with her at least weekly for 26 months. In that period of time, there had been numerous suicide attempts; a few brief hospitalizations; episodes of sexual exhibition; hundreds of hours of raucous up and down emotion, projection, black and white thinking, wild moments of rage; and brief periods of delusion, paranoia, and, on very rare occasion, frank psychosis. The meeting had gone with relative calm and good humor.

After months of back and forth, fits and starts, bickering and bargaining, trials and errors, she used the session to report that she'd finished her first week back at work in 20 years. She'd secured a job working behind the counter at a local diner. She'd been on time each day, learned the routine quickly (she was "no dummy!"), not gotten into any arguments, flirted with a few customers appropriately, and made good tips. She was proud of herself. I spent most of the session quietly validating her experience, openly expressing that there might be some frustrations in the future, but voicing that I wished her continued success in the coming week. I was pleased the session ended on an upbeat note.

I looked in the mirror to check the level of my sideburns. I needed to trim the left one just a smidgen more. I considered the path of the highways I was about to take to get to the woman's apartment in a city about an hour away. I flashed on the idea that I could get killed in an accident during the rush hour traffic on the Jones Falls Expressway. I flashed on the epitaph that might appear on my headstone at this point of life:

"He helped Cheryl Moon get a job."

It was time to consider moving on.

Practice Informed Research

When his insurance changed, his previous therapist would not continue with him.

So he had come to me referred by his previous therapist, a much older, wiser, psychiatrist. I was a much younger social worker, perhaps only a few years older than he.

He was raised in an obscure Midwestern college town where his father was a professor. It was a difficult place to be gay, and he had a profound social immaturity for a man in his late 20s. Now he had moved to a big city and become established as a competent museum archivist. He had a career. He had a nice apartment. What he did not have was friends or lovers.

Instead, he had therapy. He had been in therapy for years, since he was a child. Going to his appointment with his "shrink" each week had become more regular than going to church. As he talked in my office on a late afternoon, it was as if he was retelling a tired old script that he had told many times before. He told it in a voice that sounded like Eeyore, my least favorite character in White's *Winnie the Pooh.* He would talk that way for the next six weeks. Sometimes he would lie on the settee as if it were a couch, his long legs dangling over an arm. He gazed at the ceiling. I felt like a Freudian.

One afternoon, as he was telling the same tired tale in the same tired voice, I grew tired as I was gazing out the window. My eyelids grew heavy and drooped closed. I suppose my head bobbed a second as I jerked back into wakefulness. The patient noticed.

Resentful, which like entitlement, was a poise he played quite well. He quipped, "Am I boring you?"

I straightened in my chair. "A little, to be quite honest. I do apologize. I should be attentive, but I just get the sense you've just said this all before, many times, to many others, and quite frankly, you sound bored of it all yourself. I'm not sure where this is going to help solve your problem."

"I'm supposed to have a problem?"

"Well," I said, "I'm a problem-oriented social worker. I think I'm probably the most useful when a patient can arrive at a problem, consider a goal, and then we can try to work together for a solution, or solutions."

"Well, What do YOU think my problem is?" he asked.

I thought for a bit before responding. "Well, it's not really for me to say. But you sound kind of lonely to me."

He sat bolt upright in his chair and angrily agreed that he was lonely, but he just didn't know what to do about it. He was painfully shy. He was socially awkward. He had been to two "gay bars" in the city, but both places were sort of "rough trade" and that was not what he was about. He really didn't much like drinking anyway. He just didn't even know how to start a conversation.

I pointed out, "We're having a conversation now."

He looked condescendingly, "Oh, but that's just only because I'm paying you."

"Perhaps," I began slowly. "What we need to do is some research."

"Research?" he quizzed.

"Yes. Research. You're a scholar. You know anthropology. I've been out of the dating game for a while and I may be out of touch. I suggest you do some observational research on how people meet each other in the bar scene. Not a rough trade place. Just a nice, upscale, trendy, straight people place. There's one three blocks down from the university that seems sorta 'happening,' but safe. Take a little notebook. Sit at a table near the bar. Order a soda and something to nibble and watch how heterosexual people meet and greet each other. Take some notes and bring back what you observe, and we'll discuss it. If anybody comes up and asks about what you're doing, just tell them what you do for a living and that you're taking notes on dating behavior for a potential exhibit in the social sciences. What do you think?"

"Hmmm," he pondered, curious for the first time I'd known him, I thought. "Okay, I'll do it."

Our session started off the next week with his affect effervescent and quite animated. He couldn't contain himself. Staring me directly in the eye and smiling, "You'll never guess what happened! I met a wonderful man! We've gone out twice this week since I saw you last. His name is James and he's an architect."

"Oh?" I looked surprised. "Where did you meet him?"

"At that club you had me go to last week. I was working on the research when he came up to where I was, and we hit it off right from the start. Imagine. A gay man in a straight club! And so friendly!"

I just shrugged my shoulders. "Who woulda thunk?"

Idle Hands

Miss Mosley reminded me of a chick that had just sprung wet from an egg. She had this big ungainly head perched with a wobbly neck above a tiny scrawny body, no more than 90 pounds soaking wet. She wore large thick glasses that gave her nothing more than an ability to see lights and darks, and her hair was nothing more than a few little plats fixed with rubber bands randomly about. It was her hands that drew most of my attention. Ancient, 96 years old, dark, papery thin skin with the old bruises from some recent blood draw. And those fingers—long, long skinny little fingers that ended in wide bedded nails. She seemed so bird-like.

She was trussed in the geri-chair with two sets of body restraints, her upper torso as well as a web about her lap and tiny lower legs. Dangling from her wrists uselessly were hand restraint mitts. Her fingers picked a dime-sized hole in a plastic cushion of the chair. "She's a real Houdini," the charge nurse told me. Prior to the restraints, it was reported that she tended to slide from chairs and would be found frequently curled upon the floor, weeping.

They had called me to consult because they wanted her sedated. I did the initial assessments for my partner, Dr. Sand, the nursing home's consulting psychiatrist, and I was the gateway to neuoleptic medication. A review of her chart indicated Miss Mosley was just about deaf, almost blind, and very demented. Her long-term care now funded by medical assistance, she'd lived in a number of nursing homes in and around the city for quite some time. She had been at her present residence for just two months, a recent admission from a local hospital where she had been treated for a urinary tract infection. There was little to no social history, but there was a daughter's telephone number in a faraway town.

My contact with her was pleasant enough. I needed to yell into her left ear to make my simple comments or questions heard. She laughed simply and often and softly hummed old black spiritual hymns. We were able to get introductions understood back and forth, and simple "how are you doings" accomplished. While I interviewed her in the nursing home in the 1990s, she preferred to tell me she thought it was about 1947 and she was in a train station in Norfolk, Virginia. The president of the United States was just a little laugh and "sweet Jesus keep him safe." She was a little lady who seemed peaceable of mood and content with her sitting and singing, and picking at the little hole in the cushion, which was now worth about a quarter.

When I sat down with the floor staff, they were insistent that I get them an order for Haldol. When I chuckled and asked what could be so much fuss about this tiny deaf, blind, bird-like little old lady, they raised up a chorus of incident reports, of bad backs from picking her up off the floor, of Houdini-escapes from restraint, and destruction of property. I indicated I was a little incredulous of her powers of destruction. How could such a little thing break anything, I asked.

The charge nurse jumped up, grabbed me by the hand, and started pulling me down the hall.

"I'll show you." she said.

In a corner of the day room sat four empty geri-chairs. The vinyl of their arms, seats, and back rests had been thoroughly denuded, and the foam had been snipped out in large holes. Small metal parts like a cotter pin or an odd screw appeared to be gone. They were utterly destroyed.

"Mr. Ainsworth told me to tell you that they were all brand new and they cost $500 a chair. He wants her sedated, or out of here." She turned on her heels in a huff. I had been "showed."

I have no problem with pharmacology...indeed, my background and experiences "coming up" had led me to respect the creative use of medications in the right place, at the right dosages, for the right reasons. I liked drugs, was knowledgeable about them, and I respected their place in my toolbox of help. But I was in no rush to zonk out this little happy lady. I told the staff I was sensitive to their needs, but no new orders would be written on Miss Mosley this afternoon. I would need to call the daughter and talk with her and discuss the matter with Dr. Sand. I'd be back in the morning.

After playing some telephone tag, I was able to speak with Miss Mosley's daughter. There was some initial defensiveness in her voice, as she wondered why her mother was being seen by someone from the psychiatric team. As the conversation developed, other hints dropped here and there that seemed to indicate the daughter's great ambivalence about her mother's situation in the nursing home. She loved her mother, and wished she could take care of her, but she could not. She had children of her own, and a job, and problems with her marriage, and...well, a lot of stuff going on. As we talked, about things both central and peripheral to Miss Mosley, we got to a place where the daughter told me about what Miss Mosley was like as a younger woman, and how good she was with her hands.

Miss Mosley, it seems, had spent her life as a seamstress, and had taken care of her family by mending clothing. She mended her own clothes, those of neighbors and friends, and had many part-time jobs, and piece work from tailors and dress makers about town. Her daughter talked proudly about all the clothes she had worn as a child that had been hand made by her mother. She remarked that Miss Mosley had been skillful with many different sewing machines, and had taught her many things. There was a picture in her mind, she shared, of her mother sitting each night by a light in a parlor corner, a needle and thread in hand, mending somebody's socks or shirt or pants, or quietly doing embroidery for some friend at church. She would hum hymns quietly to herself.

It occurred to me that idle hands were the devil's playthings. Miss Mosley needed some work to do.

But what kind of work? Her dementia was so advanced, and her body so wasted and frail, that the simple instructions of folding socks or other useful work would be prohibitive. The tools of her trade, needle and thread, were long past her present abilities. The stereotypic behavior she was using to be alive was carefully tearing the fabric of expensive geri-chairs into tiny, tiny bits. What could be useful, safe, cheap, and possibly available to occupy Miss Mosley's busy fingers?

I spent much of the evening with this question occupying the back of my mind. The usual comings and goings of my young family unfolded: fixing supper, playtime, bath time, story time, bed time for bonzos (as children's hour was called). With kids nestled off to sleep, there was the couple of hours of talk, or TV, or a chapter or two of a book, before dogs had to be walked and my own night's nap could be explored. I remember plumping myself into a chair, exhaling a sigh, and turning on the TV to watch something mindless. All the time, Miss Mosley's hands kept tickling my brain.

From the kitchen, my spouse came in to remind me that I needed to call the mechanic to schedule a service for the car. I had forgotten this little job that I said I would do during the day. She threw the phone book in my lap. I wasn't sure if she was playing, or pissed...the Baltimore phone book was a big sucker, five or six inches thick and weighing close to three pounds, and it made quite a plop. I started to rifle through the pages, looking for the number of the car guy, when in my haste, I ripped a couple. Then it dawned on me.

The next morning, I talked with Shirley, the activity director at Miss Mosley's nursing home. She took care of the home's garden, and did BBC (Birthdays, Bingo, and Chapel), among other things at the home. I let her in on my idea, and she agreed. I talked with Mr. Connors, the janitor. I told him about a little problem I was about to make, and the little solution that could follow. I had always included him in my previous work at the home, asking him what he thought about this or that resident's behavior, and was careful to pass friendly time of day on occasion. He was an Orioles fan.

My last approach was to Miss Mosley, sitting in her chair. Having finished breakfast, she was quietly humming to herself, working herself out of the geri-mitts the nurses had tied about her hands. I plunked a White Pages on the table that locked her into the chair. In a few minutes, she had worked herself free of the mittens, had felt all about the large paper book in front of her, and quietly and had methodically begun tearing little pieces of paper from its pages, about the size of raisins. They fluttered to the floor one by one, like little snowflakes.

The charge nurse came out from the med room and saw me writing in Miss Mosley's chart. "Haldol?" she asked.

"No," I replied without looking up, "White Pages. We'll see how long that lasts her, and if we need to, we'll move to yellow." She looked up at Miss Mosley and gasped. A little pile of snow had dusted the floor beneath the geri-chair's wheels.

"Now, Carla," I muttered, "before you get all in a tizzie with me, let's give this a try. I've already talked with Mr. Connors and Shirley. He's cool with sweeping up the pile, and Shirley says she can use the compost in the garden. It's all just a matter of how long it will take her to get to the Zzodnicks."

"Huh?" went Carla. "Zzodnicks. Abe and Flora...they're the last name in the book. I'm pretty sure she started with the front of the book. I don't see any piece of the cover left." Carla just shook her head and walked away, probably convinced that I was just as crazy as Miss Mosley. I went back to finishing my orders. It was one of the most unique prescriptions I had ever written:

"Rx: 1 telephone book, by hand, PRN agitation."

It took Miss Mosley a little over a week to finish off a good sized edition of the Baltimore phone book. I stopped by the phone company one day and asked if I could get any old ones, explaining why. A kind lady pointed me to a huge pile in the back of the building and told me I could have as many as I could haul away. I got enough to keep Miss Mosely in the compost business for the rest of her life. Her fingers never tore up an expensive geri-chair again, and she spent the rest of her days humming hymns as her fingers did the walking through the Yellow Pages.

Happy Birthday, Eleanor

Same nursing home, different patient, same reason. "Please, please tranquilize her." Now don't get me wrong. I don't have any problems with the well-reasoned use of psychotropic drugs. It can be an absolute blessing to the poor patient who needs the right medication. I'm just not a big fan of plowing every little problem into Haldol-land unless you've looked carefully at all the particulars.

This particular was named Eleanor. A recent admission from a local hospital where she'd been treated for a fall. She'd been a resident at about four other long-term care facilities. She was an 82-year-old white female strapped in a geri-chair across from the nurses' station. The staff told me she was "just a mean old lady who needs to stop bein' so ornery." The official reason for my visit from the Attending was "consult required to assess violent patient who has injured staff and others. Possible admission to hospital gero-psych unit?" Read: "We got this patient the other day from University Hospital. We didn't know she'd be so much fuss. Get her out."

I read the chart. Nothing out of the ordinary. All the usual "little old lady" diseases, hospitalizations, and medications. Indeed, nothing acute about the apparent impulsive and violent behavior. As the patient's dementia apparently had slowly become more severe, she slowly had become more impulsive, leading to the present state of affairs in the present nursing home, presently tied down across from the nurses' station.

I watched her for a long time from a distance. She made the usual continued efforts to get free of her restraints. She would work for about 30 seconds and then stop. Relax for about 30 seconds and then start again. This would go on repetitively for about a half hour, and then she would drop her head to take a little nap for about two or three minutes. She would then awaken with a startle as somebody walked by and would yell out, "Help! Help! Help!" The somebody walking by would tell her to shush. She would try to lash out, fight against the restraints, and yell out some expletive—usually "bitch." This went on for hours. If someone tried to lean in to interrupt this process, apparently every now and again she would Houdini out of the restraints and give them a smack with an open hand.

The staff was pretty disgusted with her. They apparently tried and failed so many times that they had become frustrated and angry. This was apparent in their short tempers with her and the scowling faces they made as they passed by her in the hallway.

As I was sitting on an office chair, I began ever so slowly to inch my way across the 20 or so feet that separated us. I at the nurses' station, she in the hallway. Nothing in the pattern of behavior I had witnessed for the previous hour seemed to change much. As I got to about 15 feet from her, I saw that she would become aware of my presence, engage in the help-seeking-yelling behavior, and then drop it after about a half minute. She would drop her head and doze briefly.

I inched closer. She would awaken, be startled, and reach out for help. "Help! Help! Help!" over and over. It dawned upon me that she had a conscious reality of about thirty seconds. It was like she was walking into the middle of a new movie in a dark theater about every half minute. No wonder she was frightened. She dozed again for a minute. I smiled a big smile and inched closer and approached about six feet.

She awoke, registered me, was startled, and then smiled back. She was distracted by some other stimuli, and then looked back and started to seek "help-help-help," but then saw my smile and smiled back. For about the next 10 minutes, she was in-and-out—still with an attention span of about half a minute, but she smiled more and yelled less.

I called my supervising psychiatrist and explained my theory. In the interest of meeting the "nursing home" client, we agreed that he would call in the lightest of doses of tranquilizer, to be used at bedtime mostly.

The next morning, I arrived before the day shift came on to duty. Eleanor was already in place in the hallway, apparently after altercations with night shift much as before. While no one was looking, I snuck up behind her and silently tied a helium filled "Happy Birthday" Mylar balloon to her geri-chair. Then I pulled out a paper party hat and bobby-pinned it quickly onto her head. She didn't much notice. I then approached her slowly on my chair, smiling and waving happily.

"Happy birthday!" I said.

"Happy birthday," she echoed back. Then she would doze. Then awaken.

"Happy birthday!" I celebrated.

"Happy birthday!" she celebrated back.

The day shift came walking onto the hall, and surprised, greeting the bright balloon and the smiling, party-hatted woman. They, too, smiled and offered out, "Happy birthday, Eleanor!"

"Happy birthday!" She would wave back.

The nursing supervisor came through and was pleasantly surprised. "Happy birthday!" she smiled.

"Happy birthday!" Eleanor smiled back.

The supervisor looked at me and asked me, "What did you give her? Haldol? She's markedly brighter!?!"

"Well," I smiled a little sheepishly. "We're gonna try a little low-dose Zoloft, but mostly bump it up with a big birthday hat."

"Huh?" she quizzed. I locked her arm and started walking down the hall.

"Ms. Henry," I chirped, "let's go to your office and have a chat about this patient. I want to talk with you about the power of balloons."

Behind us, I could hear someone walking down the hall. "Happy birthday!" she said.

"Happy birthday!" Eleanor said back.

Principle of Opposites

I have read thousands of pages of books and articles on being helpful to persons in crisis and disaster. Here's what I got from all that reading—intervening in crisis requires one to stay calm and be focused on basic needs:

If cold, add warm.
If wet, add dry.
If hard, add soft.
If dark, add light.
If hungry, add food.
If thirsty, add water.
If homeless, add shelter.
If naked, add clothes.
If lost, add orientation.
If hopeless, add hope.
If crowded, add space.
If isolated, add people.

It's really not rocket science, but you'd be surprised how well it works. Walk into the middle of a crisis, stay calm, and apply the principle of opposites, and people will think you are a genius.

On the Beach

He was a man of few words.

In his late 60s, I chalked it up to his depression. His case had been transferred to me after almost a year of treatment. Examining his file, I noted that he was a toolmaker who had come to outpatient treatment after a brief hospitalization for vague suicidal ideation. Between the therapist and the consulting psychiatrist, he'd been tried on the usual array of pharmacologics without much improvement, and there had been some consideration of late of using E.C.T. His symptoms, while moderate, had been persistent.

The first sessions were torture for me. I would ask a question; he would grunt a "yes" or a "no," or a phrase of but a word or two. He was always downcast and concrete. I saw little available in him for psychotherapy and was resigning myself to be supportive but generally saw him as someone with a very "organic" depression.

I asked him if the medicine was changing his sleep, his dreaming, looking for some glimmer of improvement. He brightened just the slightest and told me that he didn't dream, but the damndest thing had happened recently—he'd had a dream that had started in recent weeks and repeated a number of nights, and he thought it was just crazy.

In the dream, he is walking along a beach and he sees a sand dollar and he picks it up. In the distance, he sees a silver dollar, and then another, and another. Collecting each in turn, he then comes upon a hole and he sees what he thinks is gold glimmering in a fathomless below. He tries reaching vainly into the hole, but he cannot reach its bottom.

He tries digging with his hands to get closer, but it is useless, as the sand just keeps shifting. He cries in frustration, and the dream always ends this way, with him waking up.

"There's something at the bottom of that hole," I said.

"I know," he said, "but I can't get it."

I asked him about the beach. Looking down at the floor, he sat silent. Then he shrugged and laid a deep sigh.

"It's Normandy—except all the bodies are gone, and I'm there all by myself."

I looked through his record. There was no mention that he had been in the Army or the war. I told him that I had not known he was a soldier. He told me that it was all a long time ago. He didn't talk about it. I asked if he ever had.

"When we got back, we were just glad to be alive. We were all tired of the war. We didn't want to talk about the war. Nobody really had anything to say that anybody should listen to."

I looked at him. "You know," I said, "given this dream, and how you feel, I think we should. Listen, I mean. Can you tell me about the war you were in?"

The man of few words began to tell his tale. He went on for seven weeks without a stop. Horror and joy. Courage, fear, greatness, pettiness, good, evil, boredom, wonder. So much gold in the hole.

All I had to do was listen.

Java time

The firefighter, FF Gabriel Morrison, sitting on the back step of Truck 8, was still probationary, but had been on the truck for about six months. He'd seen and done a lot in that time, but he stared down at his boots.

"Nothin' like this. Nothin's like this."

He'd been breaking in through the back door when debris from the second floor came crashing down and blocked him from leaving the kitchen. He could see into a dining room, and there sitting in a chair was the body of a child, perhaps no more than 10 years old, baked in the heat, arms up in a pugilistic stance. The abdomen was split open. The mouth was wide. "It was as if he was reaching for someone to help him out of this hell. I was stuck on the other side of the wall. I couldn't get to him."

"Gabe, the kid was already dead when you broke in there, right?" I asked.

"Yeah, he was crispy. But he was just a kid, and he was lookin' right at me. I couldn't do nothing. I can't get it outta my mind."

"Stop trying. Let's go to the coffee wagon. Some things stay with us for a long time."

Coffee, Tea, or Systems Theory

A few days after Hurricane Andrew, we were on the ground and headed to the Joint Services Operation Command Center. Our unit was tasked to assess and support the local and state mental health services in the aftermath of the storm. All of the commands of the federal government were assembling in a courthouse that still had most of its windows and air conditioning. The 82nd Airborne had already rung up its flag up front. We looked around to find the USPHS[6] commanding officer and took up digs in a far corner office on the second floor.

One of the first things you notice in the response and recovery phase of disaster is that there are always a lot of people doing a lot of standing around talking. I told my team, "As often as possible, sit down, and model sitting down to others. You need to conserve energy. Response to disaster is a marathon, not a sprint." When we found the Captain, we deferentially identified ourselves and asked when we report for orientation and orders. He indicated that there was no time like the present and started talking.

I asked, "Do you mind if we sit? We've been travelling a long time." There were no chairs about, so I just squatted in the hallway.

The Captain was a little surprised, but then flashed a smile and joined me, motioning to everybody to grab a knee. "Good idea," he said. "OK, let me bring you guys up to speed."

One of the other things you notice is that disaster provokes chaos, which allows for poor assessment, wasted effort, and an enormous amount of energy just organizing the simplest of tasks. The more you can identify and control the useful methods of communication and decision making in a system, the better.

The courthouse was a relatively new building—a modern 2-story box with offices lining the outer walls that surrounded courtrooms and an atrium in the center. On the first floor in a corner was a small staff kitchen that had been occupied by the 82nd Airborne. A corporal ran a huge 9-gallon coffee urn, and a doorway led out to the parking lot where people would smoke.

Bud let go a sigh when he saw it. "Great," he cheered, "at least there's coffee."

I smacked him on the back. "Not only that, but it's all in one place. That's great. We'll go find some more chairs and make this our site of informal intel and communication. Sooner or later, everybody passes through this place. This is where we buttonhole people we need to buttonhole. You don't have to go chasing all over the place to find people."

The team went about its business. Our job was to assess the community mental health infrastructure and find out what its immediate needs were in terms of human, supply, and financial resources to perform its pre-disaster services for chronic and persistently mentally ill persons, and to assess its abilities to perform disaster outreach and crisis counseling in the larger community now, and over the year to come. Additionally, we were to provide mental health consultation to any of the federal staff now serving in the emergency. A lot of work. A lot of meetings. A lot of coordination. A lot of problem solving. Doing all of this in an environment of local, state, and federal agencies all crammed into broken buildings and army tents—and few ways to communicate with each other in a day of primitive cell phone availability.

Sometime about two weeks in, the 82nd hauled down its flag and replaced it with the Stars and Stripes. The state of Florida flag now also flew. The army was continuing to play support operations, but they were consolidating their own support and logistics and relinquished some of their space in the courthouse for more state and federal human services personnel. As they "bugged out," they took their big coffee pot with them. Bud was crestfallen.

"Man, what are we gonna do?" he worried. "The Army's pulled down the coffee shop. We gotta have coffee."

I was worried for different reasons. "Bud, that's not the problem," I said. "In 24 hours, this place is gonna be awash in coffee—you won't have any problem finding Java."

Indeed, 24 hours later, in each of the little offices sat a little coffee pot serving all the needs of each of the little staffs. Bud could always find a cup of coffee. I, on the other hand, could see a threat looming on the horizon.

I ran into two sweet little ladies from the Red Cross in the courthouse lobby. They had a truck full of sandwiches and were trying to set up a point for free lunch for all the personnel responding to the disaster. I gratefully ate a couple of tuna fish on whole wheat, and asked them if they were at all in a position to assist a twenty-four-hour presence in the courthouse. I pointed out all the hungry federal and state personnel buzzing around the beehive of a building. "We all need your help; we just need a stable location so that we can find you. We need a Red Cross outreach center here!"

They called their supervisor, who upon tentatively agreeing, said I could show them the little room where the little corporal ran the coffee urn. I told them about the big coffee urn. One of them smiled and blurted, "Oh! We have an old 9-gallon urn in one of the trucks. We haven't used it in years."

"Boy, we could sure use that here!" I said.

Next morning, there was a big old "Red Cross Canteen" sign hanging outside the little room with three sweet little old ladies handing out bagels, donuts, and serving coffee from an old monster of a coffee urn. The place smelled wonderful, and a line of personnel stretched into and out of it. I saw people talking over problems. I saw this guy from the Army combat stress unit I needed to talk to.

Funny thing, the little coffee makers all over the building started to break or a part would go missing.

Per Aquam in Verbo

She was just minding the street's business from her stoop, trying to beat the August heat and feeling the weight of her pregnancy. She never heard the bullet. She thought one of the babies had kicked. There was a dull pain in her side, and then she looked down and saw the blood.

In the critical care room, the E.R. surgical resident looked down at her and explained that they would have to Cesarean deliver the babies if there was going to be any chance of saving her life. She asked if the infants would live. He said something vague about "viability," which she didn't understand, and panic raised in her eyes. Two teams from the PICU were on their way down as the woman said she was carrying twins. She looked up at the surgical resident and cried, "Don't let my babies die in sin!" She grabbed his hand. The resident looked over, confused.

"I think she wants the infants baptized," I said from the corner. Her head snapped in my direction and nodded furiously. The head E.R. Attending turned around on me and snapped, "Make it happen!"

I punched the number for the chaplain's pager and the phone rang back.

"What?!" It was the Catholic priest, and he sounded pressured. I explained to him the situation. The mother wanted baptism. He told me he was up on Seven with a family of a man who was dying and he couldn't get away. I told him the infants might be viable, but it wasn't sure for how long. I asked him what we could do.

"Are you a Christian?" he shot over the phone.

I shook. "I'm sort of a lapsed Episcopalian bordering on Buddhist, Father."

"Close enough," he shot back. "You do it. Any Christian can do it. Technically you qualify if you want to help."

"Father, we don't have any holy water," I stammered.

"Grab some sterile saline. I'll tell you what to say."

The little bodies emerged no larger than softballs. People from the Pediatric Intensive Care Unit (PICU) grabbed them and started heating them up, pumping air into their lungs and starting IVs in their tiny little limbs. I poured water on each, reciting the words the priest had instructed.

When I looked up, the woman was gone, whisked up to surgery. The tiny babies were taken up to the PICU.

Inside, I struggled. I really wasn't much of a believer in God or gods. While I personally wasn't very spiritual, I was always respectful of other people's religious traditions. In the haste of the moment, I had performed a sacrament and was quite unsure, despite the priest's directions, that I "was qualified" to perform the baptism on the two little babies. If I was unsure if I even had a soul, who was I to invoke a rite on the souls of others? I decided after a while that it was really a matter of affirming the mother's self-determination. What I believed or did not believe really didn't matter.

I learned the next day that both infants had died. My colleague up in the surgical ICU told me the mother had done well and had already been transferred to a regular surgical bed.

Some days later, I was killing time at the triage desk, having a cup of coffee and watching the people who were walking into the emergency department, keeping myself available to be helpful to some situation that might arise. She came up to the triage desk in a wheelchair, escorted by a nurses' aide. I recognized her immediately as the woman who had come through days earlier via critical care. She said she was looking for me.

We walked into the family room, and I took a seat across from her. I introduced myself, and she said, "You're the social worker. You baptized my babies."

I reached out and shook her hand. She grabbed me back and held me tightly.

I looked at her. "I'm so sorry for your loss. I'm so sorry you got shot. I hope you are feeling better. I am so sorry for your babies," I said.

"Thank you," she said, still holding my hand. She smiled weakly and had tears in her eyes. "My babies are in heaven because of you. God bless you."

I looked at her silently. I was conscious of listening. What I thought about me was not needed. We talked quietly for a little while, and then she returned up to her bed. I returned to the triage desk, watching the sun cast a shadow across the ambulance bay.

A Slice of P-I-E[7] on the Ward

My pager requested a response to the geropsychiatric unit stat. Some kind of crisis involving an agitated patient named Herb.

Herb was in his fourth day of an initial evaluation for change of mental status. He was a very tall, thin, lanky rail of a man who had retired many years ago off the docks where he had been a warehouse supervisor. In his much younger days, he'd been a star basketballer at Cardinal Gibbons High.

Coming onto the ward and looking down the corridor, I saw a knot of humanity in the middle of the hallway. It appeared that Herb had gotten out of bed against orders and had slipped on the floor. He sprawled, legs akimbo and back up against a wall, outside the door of his room. There was a hubbub all about as nurses leaned down and over him—must have been five or six, all pulling at limbs or wagging fingers. Incident report forms were already starting to appear on clipboards. Guilt, responsibility, and anger hovered. There was much shouting and resistance. "What were you doing out of bed?!" asked one. "Give me your arm!" demanded another. "Put on this slipper!" urged a third. "No No Noooo!" shouted Herb, who waved his long limbs back and forth defensively. "Now stop that! How did this happen?! Herb!" "What are you doing on the floor!?" The knot convulsed with angry answerless questions, and wasted, possibly dangerous kinesics.

Through a slip in the knot, I dove in and sat next to Herb. My shoulder to his, I sat back against the wall, and took extra moments, each with a period. I straightened my tie. I creased my pant leg. I straightened my shoe lace. I took out a pen and tapped its heel quizzically at my chin. Above and around me, the knot began to loosen and expand. I looked at Herb. Silence had attended my primping. "Well," I said, "now that we're safe and sound here on the ground, I agree with you. You do get a better view of the whole floor from here! Wot say! Should we have breakfast?"

The knot broke apart with quiet laughter and shaking heads and small smiles. Herb picked himself up with some assistance from some nurse's steady arm, and walked into his room for some grapefruit and scrambled eggs.

Stigma

It was 8 a.m. I was just about to have a cup a coffee when a secretary thrust a phone into my ear. "Come over here and look at this guy. He's one of yours and needs to be evaluated for admission." The Surgical Resident from the Emergency Department was in a hurry and hung up before I got a chance to ask a question. I was the triage officer for psychiatry that day, so I handled all the new calls for the outpatient program and had to cover the E.R.

I walked across the street to the ambulance bay and into the E.R. nursing station. "I'm from Psych," I identified myself.

"Over there, Bay 3," a busy ward clerk waved her hand and shoved a 5-inch thick medical record in my face without looking up from a pile of lab slips she was filing.

I looked over the E.R. chart on top of the record to see what I was supposed to be walking into. I recognized the name on the face sheet. I was lucky. He was a patient of mine. A guy with chronic and persistent schizophrenia who was generally cooperative and compliant with his medication. He hadn't been hospitalized since I had picked up his case about two years ago. I figured this might just be a little reactive something, and that a little supportive care and encouragement might be able to get him up, and walk across the street with me to outpatient, and then maybe a bus ride back home. Then, I noticed there was no real history on the E.R. chart, just a set of vital signs and a terse note across the section: "In from Medic 7. Found on street. Thick chart psych history. Call Psych."

My patient, Walter, a fiftyish huge black man, with the physique of middle linebacker, lay spread out on the litter, apparently sleeping. Somebody had put him in 4-point restraint. I wondered why. I had never known Walter to be violent.

I shook him at the shoe. "Walter!" I called out. Nothing. I shook again, and called again. Nothing again. I moved up to his torso and called into his ear, "Walter, wake up, it's me, Mr. Rogers." There was more nothing. If Walter was sleeping, he was really sleeping. If he was psychotic, he was really psychotic.

I smelled his breath. No alcohol. I felt his pulse—strong, regular, 78 beats per. His breath was shallow and regular, 22. I picked up an eyelid with my thumb; a pupil stared blankly at the ceiling. I popped a light at it and watched it constrict, and then dilate back to baseline. Both of his eyes did this, but left was more sluggish than right. I kept calling his name. He made no sound. I picked up his right hand and held it over his face. I dropped it and it plopped right on his nose. That almost clinched it. Just to make sure, I made a fist and rubbed my knuckles up and down on his sternum. I pinched his left nipple. Walter was unresponsive to pain. I flipped through the sheets to find the ambulance run sheet. A terse scribbled note there said he'd been picked up in an alley unresponsive, basically a scoop and swoop.

I walked back to the E.R. station and asked the whereabouts of the surgical resident. A nurse writing in a chart did not look up and asked, "You Psych? You gonna clear out the psych in 3?"

I reached out and touched her shoulder. "The patient in 3 does not need Psych just yet. The psychiatry triage officer needs to consult with the Surgical Resident. The psychiatry triage officer would appreciate it if you would get surgical resident stat. Can you help me with that?"

She shrugged me off, rolled her eyes, and huffed, "Oh jeez," and stalked off. I started to write my findings on the chart.

Just as frustrated, a bedraggled surgical resident came barreling down the hallway. "So, you gonna take your guy up to 5 or what!?"

"I'm not gonna take anybody anywhere. My guy, as you call him, is indeed my outpatient, and he might have a psych problem. But he's gotta bigger problem now, and I suggest you call your medical or neuro attending stat, 'cause the patient in 3 is out like a light, and as far as I can tell I'm the only person who's evaluated his consciousness since he came off the ambulance. And frankly, I don't think he's doin' so good. He's unresponsive to a sternal rub and a nipple pinch. His left pupil responds different from his right. Do you want to do it, or do you want me to call the Medical Attending?"

The Surgical Resident slumped his head and looked at the floor. "Sh*t," he said, "I really didn't look at him. I just thought he was crazy. I saw the psych chart and...."

"It's nada," I cut him off. "But just because they are psych doesn't mean they don't get sick or injured like anybody else. Now will you go please look at that guy? I don't know what's goin' on with him, but it looks pretty organic to me. It's just me, but I'd call Medicine and consider a neuro consult."

The surgical resident looked at me squarely. "Yep," he said, and walked down to Bay 3.

I was finishing the day about 7. Walking to the parking lot, I spied the surgical resident in the ambulance bay smoking a cigarette. He waved me over.

"Thanks for the pick-up this morning. Your guy ended up having an occipital fracture and has a bleed on the brain. He's up in ICU now."

"How'd it happen?" I asked.

"Man, I dunno. I was tired. I'd been on since 5 yesterday, and it was busy all night long...."

"No. Not you. The patient."

"Oh. Trauma. And maybe he fell, maybe somebody thumped him. I talked with the ambo guys. They didn't know anything. Anyway, it was my mistake callin' you before I looked at the guy. I just figured he was crazy."

I cut him some slack and offered my hand, "What's crazy is the hours you guys have to stand in residency."

"Yeah, you're right." He shook my hand. "It's nuts."

Malfeasance, Maldicta

The man in Bay 9 was a tall, obese, elderly white male, slowly putting his clothes on. The resident had requested I see him, as there was no reason for admission to the hospital from the E.R., but he would need to come back to the oncology clinic for an appointment on Monday.

"So?" I asked the resident, out of earshot of the patient.

"Oh, he's homeless. From Florida. He's riddled with oat cell carcinoma," came the reply. "He's probably gonna die soon."

Now fully dressed, I escorted Mr. Jessup into my office off the side of the waiting room.

Mr. Jessup had lived for several years in the alleys and park benches and occasional rooms of the east coast Florida city. He did odd jobs but mostly panhandled at times for whatever spare change would buy him wine and soothe the various demons with which he struggled. He'd sober up for a while and then slip again. He was known by the cops and the other homeless persons who inhabited the area. He made no trouble for anybody else and was known to share what little he had with others. He liked Florida. He lived by the sea.

He'd noticed the pain at first as just a small stitch in his lower abdomen that he disregarded for months. He avoided hospitals, as he had no money and no health insurance. Generally, nothing happened that he couldn't handle with a little aspirin, rest, and a little red wine.

When he couldn't take it any more, he wound up in Large Seaside Hospital. The doctors took X-rays and blood and sonograms and MRIs, and then walked up to his bedside and told him he had "the cancer." He was probably gonna die. They shook their heads and said that the social worker would come and see him.

She was a nice lady, he said, and asked about him, and all the little that he owned in the world. During the course of the conversation, he talked about his years of homelessness on the coast of Florida. She asked about his family. He told her he once had a sister who'd lived in

Baltimore. He hadn't seen her in more than 30 years. (He wasn't sure that she was even alive.) But that was enough. She never tried to track down this sister. She told him there was a world famous hospital in Baltimore. She gave him a Trailways bus ticket and the address of the Johns Hopkins hospital. He was discharged with cab fare to the bus station.

The next social worker he met was me, in the E.R., where this story started. He handed me her card. That's all he knew. He had no place to live. He knew nothing about his sister. He was a stranger in a strange city. He had no place to die. I had to help find him a place to land until Oncology Clinic on Monday.

That week, at peer supervision, I presented the case in the library of the hospital social work department. I presented the facts of the case, discussed the efforts at problem solving, and gave the latest news about the status of where the client was in terms of the plan.

"What's your assessment?" asked a colleague.

"Well, bottom line, I think this is a f***in' dump job."

"Stop right there." The departmental supervisor raised her hand at me. "I won't have that kind of language."

I looked at her incredulously. "What kind of language? 'f***in?' or 'dump job?'"

She nodded. "Either. It's unprofessional. I won't have it."

"But," I protested, furious, "that's exactly what it is—a dump job. She's dumped this client into a bus and sent him hundreds of miles away from anything he knows to our E.R., plain and simple."

"It's unprofessional," she insisted. "I won't have it."

I continued to protest. "I find your condemnation of my language oppressive. I believe you are not hearing what I am trying to say about this client's plight. This guy was given a bus ticket discharge!"

She narrowed her gaze upon me in a withering way. "I think that you don't realize you are accusing another professional colleague of an ethics violation. That is a serious action, and you better make sure you have thought through the ramifications of your blithe words."

I was shut up. I walked away from the meeting angry and ashamed.

A couple years later, I happened to be at a professional conference in Miami. Thousands of social workers had converged for the continuing education and professional socialization. There were the usual workshops and poster sessions and coffee breaks. We all smiled at each other and wore the name badges that are the ubiquitous uniform of such affairs. During a break between sessions, I noticed a woman and found myself remarking at her name tag. I remembered the name. I introduced myself and asked her if she was the she who worked at Large Seaside Hospital. She smiled and said that she was.

We chatted, and smiled, and talked about a number of concerns that we had in common. We were both medical social workers. We both worked at large receiving hospitals. We laughed over a few common stories. As the day was soon coming to an end, I asked if we might talk some more in the hotel bar, and I'd like to buy her a drink. She smiled and said she would be glad to take me up on my invitation.

"What can I get you?" I asked.

She smiled. "Oh, I feel like a vodka martini, with an olive."

I looked at the bartender and flipped a twenty at him. "I'll have a Guinness. The lady will have a vodka martini with an olive and a few choice words."

The bartender looked at me quizzically. I looked back at him and smiled. "Don't sweat it. You do the drinks. I'll do the choice words."

Drinks in hands, we toasted the happy hour. I clicked glasses and I looked at her. "Do you remember working with a homeless oat cell patient named Jessup? Well, let me tell you...."

Leaving Laundry in the Dryer: The Middles of Ends

Loretta always came in through the ambulance bay doors on a litter from Medic 7. Over a period of a couple of years, she "died" a number of times only to be revived and transferred to the ICU.

In her late 70s, she suffered from numerous chronic illnesses, the major presentation being respiratory distress as a result of congestive heart failure. There was this deep, gurgling wheeze that came from her lungs, drowning in her own fluid. Her face, lined with many years, was ashen and pale.

Rushed back into a code room, all of the nurses and residents would begin the familiar rituals of critical care. Her clothes would be cut off and dropped onto the floor. IVs, breathing tubes, and urinary catheters would be inserted. Monitors of all sort of functions would be strapped or glued on, and they would begin a symphony of beeps and boops. Blood would be drawn and medications would be injected. She would recede into this forest of elbows, necks, scrubs and lab coats, wires and tubes that encircled her diminutive frame. All around her, disconnected conversations took place that had no anchor or orientation for her.

"Gasses, stat. Somebody get me a cut down kit." "Where the heck is Respiratory?" "OK, this is gonna pinch." "Have you got lytes back yet?" "Come on people, I said nitro. I need a little nitro. What's that invert look like to you?!" "Where's radiology? Has she been flicked yet? I need a lateral, stat."

She was descending toward death's door, and all the medics in the code room were tasked on staving that off long enough to meet the requirements to ship her up to ICU. Success was not whether the patient lived or died, as long as she was alive long enough to leave the emergency room. If she died someplace else, she was still a "win" in the eyes of the young E.R. docs.

So, while everybody was doing their various physical ministrations, my job was to "be there" for Loretta. Depending on her consciousness, I would ask if there was someone she wanted to be called. I would carefully gather her things. I would touch her reassuringly. I would gaze in between the elbows and make myself available for her attention to any concern she might have. Sometimes she would mention her cat, which might need feeding, or her daughter who might be called to bring her some clothes, or could pay some attention to some bills that might need to be paid. Sometimes she would share that she was scared, or indicate her irritation that it was an inconvenient time to have a heart attack.

We had this engagement a number of times. She would arrive in the E.R., headed to death's door, and then somehow escape that moment to be transferred upstairs. In the back of my mind, I sometimes heard Groucho Marx singing, "Hello, I must be going."

One day she came in from the back of the ambulance and was in her usual state of mortal presentation. Then, despite the usual ritual of the code room, it appeared more and more as if she was "going south"—that she would finally pass on through. I am convinced she had this awareness.

She looked at me, thoughtfully, and looked beyond me. She cocked her head a bit like a dog does when it looks like it is considering the moment. Then, she smiled and gave me a wise gift. With a laugh, she squeezed my hand and said, "I've left some laundry in the dryer!" and squeezed no more.

At the end, she told me about middles.

3
The Dialogs of Hanna

In the process of a career, it is a gift to be in the company of a mentor. Social work, as a way of practice, has a myriad of nuanced skills and knowledge not easily learned from books or articles. These subtle shapes to our practice are often passed down, or gained in relationship with, a master craftsman. I strongly recommend searching for these people in life and befriending them. They will tell you important things, but often, you will grow just by watching and thinking about them.

Long ago, I heard an expression that to really own a new skill, one has to "learn one, do one, and teach one." Look for mentors, and be prepared to be one, yourself.

A Dog's Bark

The great success of dogs as a species is their capacity to live in a relationship with humans that is centered on ambiguous communication. The first wolves who ventured close enough to the humans to feed found themselves changed by the men. And the men were changed by the dogs.

What is a dog's bark? It can be an entreaty to play or a warning that soon it will bite.

"Social work is like dogs," Hanna said, "It is the profession whose utility is its ambiguity. People let us into their houses because we can be friendly visitors, but we can use our entry into their houses to hurt them as well as help them. We can be cops in sheep's clothing. The line between oppressing and empowering people is razor thin."

"So what's the trick?" I asked. "How do we keep from ceasing to be the helper and becoming the wolf?"

"The first man took a risk of a step toward a wolf, and the first wolf took a risk of a step toward the man. Somewhere in the middle, they found love and food, and that's what transformed them both."

"Wow!" I said, my head spinning with the ramifications. "Woof!"

Hanna patted Betty, the huskie at his feet. "Exactly!"

Strengths Perspective

Hanna said:

"Let me tell you about social work."

"Some people walk down the sidewalk and they see a dog turd. When they see that dog turd, they turn their nose up at it. Maybe they make a face, a frown, a scowl, scrunch up their nose, maybe even look away from that dog turd. They shake their head and they blame whoever put it there. If they have stepped in that turd, they get real angry. They yell 'sh*t!' and try as fast as possible to scrape that turd off their shoes. They do their best to get away from that turd as fast as possible."

"But a social worker, she'll come right up to that turd and really look at it. She will pick it up and feel its heft. She will ask questions: How heavy is this turd? How much moisture does it hold? Is it dark brown or a little light brown? Is this turd still warm? What can you do with this turd? Could you use it for fertilizer to grow nice flowers? Would somebody consider paying money to buy it? How could this turd make the world a better place? This, this is some good sh*t!"

The Tao versus the Art of War

Hanna and I were jogging away from the hospital. We had worked our way through a wooded trail past the museum and were heading up a hill and more open country. It was only our second mile, and I was already huffing.

"I'm studying the Tao," I said. "'The sharpest knife cuts no bone.' Lao-Tzu,[1] I think."

"Ach-hoo!" said Hanna, "Boo-Hoo! Social workers would be better to study Sun-Tzu."[2]

I puffed. "But I think they're complementary. They both would appreciate not forcing things."

Hanna picked up his pace, leaving me behind. "Sun-Tzu would have kicked Lao-Tzu's ass."

First, Kill All the Lawyers[3]

Part One

Hanna once said: "Nothing is more dangerous than a clinical meeting with only one psychiatrist in the room, except any meeting with only one lawyer in the room."

Part Two

I was ticked. I had a difficult case that I had worked weeks on. The client had a very complex problem that had many unanswered questions. I had successfully arranged for a number of special services to be provided, only to be told to cease my efforts. My supervisor told me I was not to provide any more extra efforts on the client's behalf. The agency's lawyer said the extra effort had put the agency at liability of not being able to meet future expectations of the same level of service. I fumed.

Hanna kicked his feet up on my office coffee table and stretched his arms behind his head. "Our lawyers are guys who do not make their living taking people to court. Lawyers who do not make their living taking people to court live their lives being afraid of lawyers who do."

"So?"

"So, they spend all day making policies that protect people from litigation. The policies aren't law. Our lawyers are afraid of law. If they had their way, everybody would be wrapped up in so much bubble-wrap that nobody could say or do anything for anybody. Which is okay, because once the system gets so stopped up, a client gets angry and gets one of the lawyers who do make their living taking people to court, and then some of the bubble-wrap goes away for a while."

Part Three

I flopped down on Hanna's couch. "God, I hate lawyers!"

Hanna laughed. "Grasshopper, lawyers are the social worker's best friend."

"Whaaa?"

The laughter continued. "Lawyers spend every day looking to make black-and-white in the world. They have these things they love called 'bright lines' where black falls on one side and white falls on the other. But the minute they make a bright line, someone, sometimes another lawyer, often just Joe Schmoe on the street, finds out the bright line has some smudges of gray in it. Gray is where social workers live. Somebody's got to take care of people who fall into the gray."

"I never thought of it that way."

Hanna just smiled. "We'll always have jobs. They keep making black-and-white, which always just makes more gray."

Part Four

"They told me not to ask the client anymore about his special problem. It's not our concern."

Hanna fiddled with the telephone cord. "So, do what you're told in spades."

"Huh?"

Hanna frowned. "Were you asleep during the lecture on Alinsky?[4] One of the Rules for Radicals was to 'make the enemy live up to its own rules.'"

"OK. I heard that one. But I don't see how it applies."

Hanna sat quietly and thought for a while. "One of the things I do with a couple who come to see me for sexual counseling is tell them to stop having sex. I tell them between now and our appointment next week, under no circumstances are you to have sex."

I looked at the client. "I need to tell you something right from the beginning of this session. My agency has specifically prohibited me from asking you anything about your special problem. Under no circumstances can I ASK you about it."

The client smiled a big smile.

F***ing Swiss Cheese

Darby rushed into her supervisor's office in a panic.

That afternoon she had done an initial interview with a man who had been referred by his primary care physician for depressive symptoms. During the interview, he indicated that one of his problems was that he was having sex with Swiss cheese.

"I don't know what do to do!" cried Darby. "How can I possibly help this guy?"

Hanna sat like a cat in a sunlit corner, reading a book by Patrick O'Brian[5] that he had read before. He chewed on the stub of an unlit pipe between teeth in the corner of his mouth. He had taken it back up in these later years, but permitted himself just one bowl, which he enjoyed over a morning coffee and a walk around the neighborhood of the clinic.

"Hmm." His eyes did not leave the pages but his eyebrows raised. "Cold cheese? Warm cheese? Does his cheese have a name? How long has he had sex with cheese? Where does he do it with the cheese? In the bedroom? The kitchen? Does anybody watch him? Does he dress the cheese up? How, exactly, does he have sex with the cheese? Why is cheese better to have sex with than other things? How is it, exactly, that he thinks he has a problem because he has sex with cheese?"

Darby looked down at the floor. "I don't know," she said.

"Well, you better find out," Hanna said. "Come back and tell me and we'll talk more."

Two weeks later, during supervision, Darby discussed the case. She was much calmer and reflective. "It's a very interesting problem. I never thought there might actually be good reasons for having sex with cheese."

Hanna's Rule

Hanna said:

"As shaky as my cosmology might be, it does have some absolutes. Understand this: the number of assholes in the universe is a finite proportional constant. When one dies, another is born to take his place, and X number of new ones are born as the population of the world increases."

"There are two other groups of humans: good people and competent people. Some people are just good. Some are just competent. Some people are both good and competent. Some are both competent and assholes. You have to really watch those guys. There are also some folks who are both good and assholes. They are dangerous in a whole 'nother way."

"The fundamental purpose in life is for the good and competent people of the world to find each other and work to mitigate the harm done by the assholes."

"There is a codicil to this rule," he went on.

"I'm the biggest asshole I know."

Force Continuum

I was really pissed.

Hanna simply replied, "Don't burn the village if you only want to cut the grass."

"Huh?"

"Theory of escalation, bud. A battle can turn into a war, or end in a minor skirmish. A military approach argues for the use of proportional force to accomplish the mission objective."

"Huh?"

"Look, you're pissed. Act not, outta being pissed. Act only out of accomplishing your objective. Start informal and move only to formal if informal does not accomplish your goal."

"Huh?"

"Jeez louisee," he hung his head. "Take the rest of the night to emotionally obsess about this until you get bored with yourself. Once you can get rational, then plan an action based upon force continuum. In the morning, ask him if he's gotta minute and talk this out informally. If it can't be resolved, then and only then, move to paper. Paper ups the ante for him and for you, 'cause the rules require him to respond in kind. Paper means written down things might be read by other people. Paper means ideas get fixed in time and space. Paper means lawyers could get involved. First, deal with the guy informally. If that doesn't work, then you talk 'formally.' You say, 'This is a formal complaint I am making orally.' Then wait and see what happens. If nothing happens, then go to a formal written complaint to him—again, wait and see. At the bottom of the memo, write some bullsh*t like 'cc to file.' If nothing happens, then go to oral complaint to his supervisor. Then go to paper with his supervisor, and so on. But don't go to the boss on paper without first letting things rumble a little bit in the jungle. And only rumble if you've thought through why your passions are in an uproar, and what solution you really want."

I looked at Hanna. "I really just wish I could use a rocket launcher on the guy."

Hanna looked back. "Yeah, those things are fun, but they make a hell of a mess."

Alphabits

Hanna and I were watching the Eagles lose to Dallas again. We were well into a hopeless 3rd quarter when he stated non-sequiturally, "I think it began with CPR."

"Huh?" I replied.

"CPR...ya know, cardio-pulmonary resuscitation."

"OK," I said, "I'll bite...what started?"

He looked over his beer. "This tendency to put everything that has to do with helping people into little sweet packages with initials. So it sounds likes it's all-so-more scientific than it probably really is. Like CBT."

"Oooof," I noted. "And RET, DBT, TFT, EMDR."

He nodded. "PTSD, BPD, OCD, NGO."

"LSMFT."

"Wha?"

"Lucky Strike Means Fine Tobacco," I said, confidently.

Hanna smiled, deviously. "We should make one up and sell it. Maybe we could get SAMHSA[6] to make it an empirical best practice—an EBP."

"OK, I got one. A poor person comes in and you give them some money. That's RPT, Resource Provision Therapy."

"Booya," Hanna cheered. "Howabout a guy in crisis comes in and says he's lost. You sit him down. Find out where he's trying to go and you give him directions. POI. That's Postural Orientation Interviewing!"

"Brilliant!" I said. "Once again, we've made the world better whilst the Eagles have lost another game."

"SNAFU," said Hanna.

"SNAFU," I replied.

Teleology and Deontology?

I paraphrased Alinsky: "The people concerned with means and ends wind up on their ends without any means."

Hanna shrugged. "People unconcerned with means toward ends wind up with mean ends."

In the Middle of a Football Game

At half-time, the Eagles were getting trounced by the Cowboys.

"I've been really struggling with the difference between Private and Public. When does public concern end and private responsibility begin? When people talk about freedom, what do they really mean?"

Hanna threw Betty a corn chip. "Yeah, I've been fussing with the difference between production and consumption. When people talk about Labor and Capital, what really is the difference? Does everything in life have to be a commodity?"

"Woah," I said. "Too much for half-time. I really hate the Cowboys."

"I hate the Cowboys, too," said Hanna.

Supervisory Ruling

"So I have this client," I said, "and I'm not sure if he's eligible for services. I looked at the rules, and he seems to fall into a crack of the regulations. Do you think I should ask Walter about it?"

Hanna shrugged. "Does the client need the services?"

"Yeah. So?"

Hanna shrugged again and raised his eyebrow. "Does the client need services?"

"Yes. I already said..."

"Asked and answered, Your Honor, may it please the court!"

Frustrated, I started again. "Look, all I want to know is if..."

Hanna cut me off again. "I know what you wanna know. I know that I don't wanna know what you wanna know. I especially don't wanna know what our supervisor might rule on what you wanna know."

"Huh?"

Hanna sighed, "Never ask for an interpretation from a higher authority unless you are prepared to live with an adverse ruling. It is easier to seek forgiveness than it is to seek permission—just don't violate the Martens Clause."

"What's the Marten's Clause?" I asked.

"Look it up. Just don't do anything that violates the laws of humanity or the dictates of the public conscious. Geneva Conventions.

"Wow. I thought they only applied in time of war."

Hanna shrugged. "It is always a time of war."

The Difference Between Smart and Right

I was pissed again. Some unjust policy had appeared at work out of nowhere, with what I thought were poorly considered reasons.

Hanna munched a sandwich. "In war, the smart pick the right battles."

"Huh?"

"Don't stand in front of a tank unless you're prepared to die or have a Plan B."

"Huh?"

"Dead is for a long time. Plan B lets you live to fight another day, and there's always the chance there's another day."

"Huh?"

"OK. Lookit. There's a time to be right, and there's a time to be smart. Wisdom is knowing when it's right to be right, and when it's right to be smart. Sometimes you can be right, but not smart, and you lose. Sometimes you can be smart, and it's really not right. It's best to be right and smart at the same time, which does not happen often."

"How do I figure out when it's right to be smart, and when it's smart to be right?"

Hanna leaned back, looking out the window at some beautiful clouds passing in the sunny afternoon. "That, you have to figure out for yourself. And the wisdom will not make you happy."

The Philosophy of Science

Hanna peered over his beer at me. "Nietzsche[7] says God is dead."

I looked back. "Nietzsche is dead."

Hanna peered again at me. "Hmmm," he said.

I looked back. "So, both God and Nietzsche are dead."

Hanna pondered out loud: "We have no evidence that God is alive or dead. But there is clear evidence that Nietzche is dead. According to SAMHSA's rubric, God might be considered a 'promising practice,' but dead Nietzche is an 'Empirically Based Practice.' Grant money-wise, dead Nietzche trumps God."

I peered over my beer at Hanna. "We should come up with an acronym."

Hanna looked back. "D.N.T. Dead Nietzche Therapy. Sounds like a winner."

"I like it," I said. "Let's write it up. We'll get published in *Social Work*."

"Nah..." said Hanna, "They'd never understand the regression analysis."

Literary Criticism

Looking over the books in my library, Hanna observed, "I see both *The Fountainhead* and *Atlas Shrugged*. You were once an aficionado of Ayn Rand?"[8]

"As an undergraduate, I flirted with Objectivism. Just, I might add, as I flirted with Mao and Marx, and Communism."

Hanna sniffed. "I flirted with Wendy Smith. She rocked my world. And then she shrugged."

"Hanna," I declared, "Surely you must have at least respected Rand's articulation of the creativity of the human spirit in the character of Howard Roark?"

"I think she ripped every idea she ever had off of Nietzsche, and aggrandized herself to make a profit off of it."

"Well, she probably would have agreed with you a bit there. But you have to admit she was quite an individual."

"In the end, she took the Medicare to pay her hospital bills, and cashed the Social Security check just like everybody else. How lucky for her that the collective still supported her individuality in her time of dependence."

Hanna Shrugged.

Yet More Literary Criticism

Hanna noticed on my bookshelf, "Ah, Whitman's *Leaves of Grass?*"[9]

"I too am not a bit tamed—I too am untranslatable;
I sound my barbaric yawp over the roofs of the world." I replied.

He looked at me, raising his glass in respect.

Thus in silence in dreams' projections,
Returning, resuming, I thread my way through the hospitals,
The hurt and wounded I pacify with soothing hand,
I sit by the restless all the dark night, some are so young,
Some suffer so much, I recall the experience sweet and sad,
Many a soldier's loving arms about this neck have cross'd and rested,
Many a soldier's kiss dwells on these bearded lips.

"I like Leonard Cohen,[10] too," I said.

The glass was raised again.

Oh like a bird on the wire,
Like a drunk in a midnight choir
I have tried in my way to be free.

Changing the Rules

It was Friday and I had spent all the lunchtime grousing about crap that had happened at work. I remember that there had been six or seven directives that had come from the Director's office that I had spent all week trying to catch up on. It seemed like just when I was beginning to see daylight, another thing came heaping down. The rules, it seemed, on the workload were changing. Lots of folks were nodding their heads in agreement, as we picked at our food.

After lunch, it was our custom to play ping-pong. A table was set up in the play-therapy room. One end was a little short against the wall, but that wall was all clear. The other end gave the player more room to move, but it was filled with all the clutter and toy boxes of the therapy room. Losing the ball on that end usually meant a search.

Hanna was much better than I, with years of practice, but I was learning his game and improving with every contest. As I was the lesser experienced, I usually took the short side first. "Nope," Hanna shouted. "New Rules—I get short side first."

Game one Hanna had the short end and he skunked me, 6-0. I was "cold" and not ready for the game. It was also not uncommon for Hanna to skunk me. We switched sides.

I aced two in a row from the start. Hanna picked up the third point on what seemed like an endless volley, both of us laughing. "Good point," I conceded to him. Another ace, and then I picked up a short volley with a change-up lob. I was feeling confident as the serve changed to Hanna. He came up wicked, but faulted. He got frustrated with the next points and made some position mistakes. I played relaxed and stayed on top. I pulled off a mid-skunk at 12-1. Hanna slammed his paddle. "Best two out of three," he glowered. "I've got short side."

We switched sides. "Loser serves," I announced, flipping the ball across the net. Hanna smacked it back. "No. New Rules. Winner serves." He seemed pissed. I felt a little confused, but agreed to serve.

Ace. Ace. Ace. Hanna slammed his paddle and cursed. "I don't have it today." Ace. Ace. My serve was on fire. I was smiling. Hanna took the ball. He took a breath, and then gave the ball a toss, then a slice with the paddle. It was brilliant, but wide. "Fault!" I called "Not off the end." I scurried through the puppets box to get the ball and tossed it back to Hanna. I got set, expecting another smash to the corner. He looked like it would be furious, but then switched up and laid a little dribble across the next. "Yours," I called out. "1-5."

The game fell back into my hands and I scored the next six points, heading for another mid-skunk. At what should have been my 12th point, we had another one of the endless volleys that ended with Hanna's smash flashing low and off into a cluttered corner. I dug around on my hands and knees looking for the ball. "Well, you beat the skunk, anyway," I said.

I never got another point that service. The rest of my serves ended coming back, always out of my reach or expectation, with the ball flashing into some hidden recess of a toy box or the clutter of a corner. Hanna's frustration had melted away, and a Cheshire cat smile replaced an earlier fixed frown. Ping. Pong. Point after point, long volleys, short volleys, aces. Everything ended up with me in a corner rummaging around for a ball. I would pick up a point, but almost as an afterthought. I suspected a deliberate flub on Hanna's part. He made up all his lost ground while I was dripping with sweat chasing lost balls. We finally got to 20-all.

"I gotta patient next hour," I said, "Howabout new rule, next point is winner?" "Nope," Hanna smiled back, "gotta win by two." I took the next point. "Game!" I declared. "Nope," Hanna just smiled, "gotta win by two." And then it began. His point, my point. His point, my point. Only my point was clearly calculated on his part, and his point was drilled into some clutter of dolls, finger paints, and fire trucks. My pants were a mess. It went on for what seemed like another half hour.

"You sh*t," I sputtered, "you're playing me. Just play the game and win." He laughed. "I am. Ah...That was your point, and it's your serve. Can you get the ball outta the corner?"

He took the next point, tying again with another humiliating smash to a far corner. I had it. I threw my paddle down and snarled

"That's IT! I'm not pickin' up that damn ball again. I've got a patient to see and real work to do."

"New rule." He gazed back meeting my eyes level and clear. "You win."

I fumed as I stormed down the hallway to my office to get ready for my appointment. As I "cleared my decks," it dawned on me, and I started laughing quietly. I knew on that Friday what topic I would bring to my agenda for supervision. I was not picking up the ball again.

Hiccups

It was Friday, and we all went to happy hour at the bar down the block from the clinic. It had been a long week, and everybody was eager to unwind and tell what tales that could be told from the secrets of the therapy office, draped, of course, in the confidentiality that confessional demanded.

Not surprisingly, midway into my second beer, I got the hiccups. I had the floor at the time and was frustrated by the interruption provoked by my irritated 10th cranial nerve. The table laughed.

Hanna sat next to me and took the spotlight. "I can cure you of the hiccups hypnotically, if you'd like."

"Yeah. Sure," I said, waving him off.

"No, really. I can," he smiled. "It won't hurt. I promise." All around the table looked on eagerly. Some nodded seeking to encourage me.

"Okay, erp, okay," I acquiesced.

Hanna began. He asked everyone at the table to be quiet for a moment. He leaned into me and put his arm around my shoulders. He talked softly into my ear.

"Now listen to me, and understand what I am about to say. Everything that is about to happen is in your control and never once will you be in harm or danger. At no point in time will you be afraid, or need to fear anything. Everything that is about to happen is something that you will do or not do based only upon your decision to do it. I will only make suggestions. You are always in control, and I am only your friend making suggestions. If you follow my suggestions, your hiccups will cease. Are you ready?"

I nodded. I hiccupped.

Hanna pointed to the wall of the bar. "Up there on the left, is the head of a moose. It's stuffed and mounted on the wall. Do you see it?"

I nodded. I hiccupped.

"If you see it, say 'yes,'" he said.

"Yes." I hiccupped.

"Over there, on the right, there is a branch and a stuffed bird. It's an owl, I think. If you see it, say 'yes.'"

"Yes." I hiccupped.

"Now, listen to me carefully. Remember that this is about you being in control. For some strange reason, over there on the wall, someone has mounted an old typewriter. Between the moose head and the owl. I want you to look at the moose and focus upon it."

I did. I hiccupped.

"Now I want you to focus upon the owl."

I did. I hiccupped.

"Now slowly, back and forth, I want you to look at the moose, and then upon the owl, and then upon the moose again. I want you to alternate your focus back and forth steadily between the moose and the owl."

I hiccupped. I looked at the owl, then the moose, then the owl. I hiccupped again. Everyone at the table had become silent and intent upon me. Only the noise of the bar could be heard in the background.

"Do that for a moment or so and then, remembering the typewriter between them, keep alternating your gaze, and make up a story about both the owl and the moose. Make up a story while you are shifting the focus of your eyes back and forth. Make up the story with a beginning, middle, and end. It doesn't have to be a complex story. It can be simple. It can have no particular meaning. But it must be a story about the moose and the owl, while you are alternating your gaze back and forth between them. When you are ready, keep shifting your eyes, and begin to tell us the story."

I looked at the moose, and the owl. The owl and the moose, then the owl, then the moose. I considered that they were both animals in the forest. I looked at the owl. I considered that one day the owl had been shoved by the wind and struck a tree, hurting his wing, and he could not fly. I looked at the moose. I considered that the moose came along and found the owl walking and offered to carry him to a place where he could get his wing healed. I looked at the owl. I considered that the owl forever appreciated the kindness of the moose and for the rest of his life would tell the story of how kindly a moose can be to owls. I looked at the moose.

I looked at the moose, and began to tell the story I had just made up. I looked at the owl. I got as far as telling about how the owl had hurt his wing when I noticed that everyone was listening to me intently with open mouths. I noticed my hiccups were gone.

I insisted that Hanna tell me how he had done it. He refused, laughing. "You never give away magic."

Some years later, I saw Hanna again at a conference. I invited him to the hotel bar and we talked about how things were going at the old agency. I had moved on to a big city hospital. He had gone on to a private practice. After a while, I reminded him of the hiccup episode.

"Ah, the juggler's hypnosis," he said. "I used to do that all the time. It's really quite simple. The conscious mind can only perform so many tasks at once. It's a great way to block things like panic, phobia—works for hiccups, too. You get the client to focus back and forth on some objects, get them to make up a story about the objects, all the while you're telling them that they are in control and that they will relax, or their hiccups will go away. They've got so many cognitive balls in the air they can't keep up with the unwanted symptom."

I felt satisfied. I had suspected that some kind of cognitive confusion was the source of the cure. I went on for some years curing hiccups in bars using Hanna's "juggler's hypnosis" technique.

Many years later, out of nowhere, on the telephone message recorder in my university office was a very cryptic voice message. "This is Hanna. I never give away the magic."

I futilely tried for a few days to call Hanna. He was never in his office. I left messages on his machine. I tried calling the coffee shop he and his third wife ran in a far away city. The barista on duty said he could take a message. I forgot about talking with Hanna after a while.

One day after lunch, I was on my way to class, in a hurry as I was going to be late. I noticed I had the hiccups. I hustled into the classroom and began to boot up the computer and the overhead projector for my lecture—a process that always seemed to take about five minutes. I noticed that my hiccups were gone. I hadn't been particularly busy in my mind, as the computer process before a lecture had become an auto-pilot routine for me. It dawned upon me.

After class, I went rummaging around in my files until I found an old e-mail address for Hanna. I fired off a message: "You old fart! I figured it out. Anybody's hiccups probably only last so long. The whole shifting eyes and story thing is just a bogus distraction—a time-waster—making people give you responsibility for something that's going to happen anyway!"

My telephone rang a few minutes after I hit "send." It was Hanna. "I'm glad you finally got it. Now that you're a teacher and all. One never gives away the magic."

And he hung up.

A Halloween Story

It was Halloween afternoon and I was trudging through the tedium of paperwork when the phone rang. I thought I recognized the voice.

"Like Likes Like, but Difference is the seed of Reality."

I laughed. "Why, yes, you are correct. It's important to consider similarities with a client to help reduce the sense of social distance and defensiveness. It's useful to consider a little mimesis with a client's posture, narrative expression, and 'begin where the client is' in the beginning of a relationship. It helps a client to begin with a helper who is somewhat like him."

"That being said," I continued, "It is also important to have a real sense of yourself. To be a real presence in the relationship who can model tolerating where two people are different; who can be a real object for the client to bounce off of, and in so doing allow them to discover more about themselves!"

"But, Otto Rank,[11] you've been dead since the 1930s! Hanna, you dog, is that you?"

The voice on the phone rebutted, "Hanna? Who's Hanna?"[12]

And hung up.

4
Ends

So much about life in western civilization is about acquisition-getting, buying, learning, doing, birthing. Very little effort in our culture is spent considering the ends of things—stopping, reflecting, losing, mourning, and dying.

The wise social worker is one who knows the importance of boundary. In knowing where the limits are, one can be free to move within and up to them. Perhaps, even surpass them. But without acknowledging the ends of things, so much of beginnings and middles can just be unawakened experience. Endings can be a time of sadness or celebration; rage or triumph; prepared for, worked toward, or sheer surprise. It may be impossible to see beyond the horizon, but for any vision, there is a vanishing point. We must respect the power of the ending of things.

The 9th Inning

He only pitched one year in the Carolina League. He claimed he got a base hit off Babe Ruth during an exhibition game and struck him out. The Babe still played for the Red Sox then.

I was a second-year student in the geriatric clinic.

He was 89. At night it would become worse, an anxiety that would shake him to his core. He would stumble out of his apartment and just pace up and down the long corridor of the senior high-rise. His neighbors did not know what to do and they did not like it. The management of the building was making rumblings that he needed to be hospitalized. I had seen him twice a week for two weeks, and it was not getting any better. He had no family. He had no friends. He had lived alone for years. It was the "fear and trembling and sickness unto death."

The psychiatrist I took him to at the university hospital said he was an interesting case, but did not need hospitalization. He spent half the time talking baseball. He wrote him scripts for a sedative and an anxiolytic, and told me he obviously had a good relationship with me and to keep seeing him twice a week in the building's clinic. I should reschedule in a month. That was a Friday.

On Tuesday, he did not come down for his appointment. I went up and knocked on an unresponsive door. I got the building manager and said I thought he might be very sick. Could we open his apartment immediately?

He lay on the bed quite clearly dead, perhaps for a couple of days. I called down to the clinic for the doc and asked him to come up.

"Is he dead?" he said.

"It looks that way to me."

"Call 911 and ask for the cops and an ambulance. Wait there until the cops come and tell them I'll do the paperwork. They can come down to the clinic to get it."

"Do you want to get an autopsy?" I asked. "I think it's possible he mighta OD'd. He was just put on some new tranqs, and there's a half bottle of vodka on a table nearby."

"No. He had heart disease. I'll do the certificate."

I persisted. "I feel kinda bad about this. I set this guy up with treatment, and I might have killed him. If we got an autopsy, I'd know for sure."

The doc insisted, "Look. Didn't you tell me he pitched Babe Ruth?"

"Yeah."

"Then he was 89 years old and had a heart attack. You did what you could. That's all you and me and anyone else needs to know—and he pitched Babe Ruth."

Single-Subject Design

She worked with some of the most difficult patients I know. Deeply listening and reaching into the places from which they feared. She found sunshine within them and courage to forge their own stronger paths. She was very good at what she did. Having been a student of mine many years earlier, I came to know her as a master.

She eschewed evidence based practice and once told me that she had a voice from "the universe" that visited her from time to time. She listened to the heart, she said. We were having an argument over the need to practice accountably.

"You once told me that science, based upon the normal distribution, can never predict for the individual. I begin and end with the dignity and worth of the person. Everything else flows from there. I practice a science of the unique; an art of compassion."

I had no evidence, nor heart, to refute her.

In Memory of Louise

In that weekend of January during my freshman year, my school was still in recess but she had returned to hers. With a luxury of time, I drove the old VW microbus across the turnpike and, after hours, turned north from Pittsburgh into the frosted western Pennsylvania country where her college would be nestled against a small mountain and low gray clouds.

On the way, I stopped into a diner for some soup and coffee. Some small town south of Slippery Rock. As I ate at the counter, I looked to my right at a man eating a sandwich. "Excuse me sir," I asked the man. "Are you Mr. William Windom, the actor?" The man nodded, still chewing his sandwich. The actor indicated he had been doing a play in a nearby college theater. "I always liked you in *The Farmer's Daughter*," I said. "It was a shame about Inger Stevens."[1] Mr. Windom nodded again and said, "She was beautiful, but sad."

***

For my sixth birthday, my grandmother had sent me some paper money. It must have been something like five dollars, a fortune. My mother told me my grandmother wanted me to buy a birthday present for myself. I asked my mother if we could go up to the Grant Company store and buy some fish. It had been one of the wonders of my world to walk into the back of the Grants, a virtual zoo, filled with big tanks of swimming fish, hamsters, mice, and cages of squawking birds.

I quickly learned that my money would not go as far as I hoped. I could not purchase a tank, some fish, and all the things needed for their care for my five dollars. The man at the back of the store told my mother numbers that were well outside of my reach. I grew disappointed, and I'm sure it showed on my face. He was not without effort, however, as he pointed out that for my money I could get a turtle, a bowl, a little plastic palm tree, and some turtle food. He showed me the turtles, little green and black bottle caps, swimming about in a few shallow inches of a tank in the corner. I was happy and excited to select one. I called him Tommy.

***

In the November before this visit, I had taken the Greyhound down to her family's house outside of Washington, D.C., having been invited for Thanksgiving break. Snow fell as the bus pulled into the terminal, and I saw her waiting excitedly at the dock, dressed in a Navy pea-coat and signature curly wild hair.

After dinner, I joined her as her parents had asked her to walk the family dogs. The snow that had begun earlier was now falling in large wet flakes. The dogs were oblivious except to their business. I, on the other hand, was mad to receive all the sensation surrounding. The sound of muffled tires on Connecticut Avenue. The sparkling circles of snow shimmering from the streetlights like a Van Gogh painting. The weight of the snow on the shoulders of my stadium coat. The warmth of her mittened hand in mine. The smell of wet wool mixed with the slightest hint of Pachouli. I was conscious in that moment that I would never forget this simple little walk through Chevy Chase streets on a winter night.

***

Tommy the turtle lived in a sunny corner of my bedroom. I had searched for, found, and scrubbed, just the right selection of flattish rocks to build a little island in the middle of the bowl. The plastic palm tree grew upon the rocks, and taped to one side of the bowl I had used crayons to make a picture of clouds and sky and ocean, and other happy turtles smiling at Tommy.

I had gotten some books from the library on turtles. Some I could read, but most I could only understand from the pictures. I learned how to feed Tommy and keep his shell clean. I learned what food to feed him, and how to clean the water in his bowl. I learned that sometimes he was active and sometimes he was sleeping. I learned that he could tuck his head into his shell. I learned that Tippy, our dog, was very interested in him and would try to sniff inside his bowl. Tommy told me he did not like Tippy.

***

When I got to her college, I was a little shy, and polite, and pre-pared to crash in a male dorm. But she arranged to have her roommate away, and she secreted me into her room. We talked and had coffee and cookies for what seemed like hours talking about the most trivial things.

With her friends, we had pizza and went to the movie in town. The film, *The Way We Were*,[2] was too close for me. There was an awkward-ness about her as well. She was Katie and I was Hubble. The Jewess and the very Gentile.

In the morning, she went for an exam. I stayed on her bed and read a book I knew would come for the next semester. When she returned she was crying. She was not to be consoled but recovered after a time as she helped me pack up. She kissed me on the cheek and said good-bye, and then walked over to a tree as I started up the microbus. Cold, brilliant air twinkled in the morning sunlight. The snowy mountain behind showed her almost in silhouette against the tree. I could see her face in shadow. Tears had frozen on her cheeks and her face was sad and angry. She smiled weakly.

I knew we would never be lovers again. And the vision of this good-bye would be with me forever.

***

One morning Tommy the turtle looked different. His face was cov-ered by a gauze of mucus and his shell had a yellowish cast. He moved stiffly and slowly. He did not eat. I changed his water and prayed and prayed before going off to school. When I came home, I found him floating, dead. My mom helped me wrap him in toilet paper and put him into a shoebox. I buried him near a pine tree next to the garage in our backyard.

Later that night, alone in my room, I began to sob. My mother came in and asked me what was wrong. I told her how awful I was to let Tommy die. I was sure that I had done something wrong. If only I had fed him vitamins, or different food, he would not have become sick. I was responsible for his death and my heart ached. She stroked my forehead and assured me that I had done nothing wrong. But I cried until I fell asleep. I never got another turtle.

***

I was in Vancouver last year giving a lecture to oncology social workers when I learned that she had died. I remember her as being the most sympathetic with patients who had cancer. Her mother had died of cancer, she told me, and she thought it was one of the worst diseases. It was a cruel irony to hear that she had died from the disease. Throughout this past year, I have found myself thinking of her, and missing her in the world. Captain Louise Meister, USPHS, was my field instructor.

What I first remember about Louise is that everything about her was large. On a spring time many years ago, framed in silhouette against an office window in the USPHS Hospital Baltimore, I was interviewed for my first placement by two officers in the social work department. Louise was tall and angular, with severe features. Piercing eyes, arched brows, long arms with prominent elbows, she leaned forward in the interview and seemed very crone-like and menacing. Her colleague Andy was ex-Army Medical Corps, jocular, and physically taut. He worked hard to put me at ease and laughed a lot. I remember little concerning the interview except that about halfway through, I wondered if they were playing "bad cop-good cop" with me. Louise would ask questions I felt intimidated by, and Andy would easily accept my nervous answers. I was relieved and happy when some days later, Andy called me on the telephone and indicated they had accepted me for the placement, and that he would be my supervisor. I enjoyed my summer and looked forward to my field assignment in the fall.

I was surprised on my first day to be told by Louise that things had changed. The department had accepted another student, a BSW, who would be supervised by Andy. As I was the MSW placement, Louise as the senior officer would supervise me. I was crestfallen.

I was not the easiest student. I've long been bright and very book smart. As an undergraduate, I was a willful student who had learned to learn despite my teachers, who for the most part couldn't teach me anything in my arrogant little opinion. I was, and have always been, a voracious reader and filled my head with the things from books. Teachers in my then young view were often people who got in the way of my wanting to know things.

When she suggested we co-lead a group for young Coast Guard recruits who were in the hospital to have their wisdom teeth removed, I was incredulous. What could possibly be the benefit of a one-shot group for young guys who were just having dental surgery? But week after week, I became amazed as she opened the door for these young men to share and struggle with a deep host of human concerns. Their disappointment of having been pulled from boot camp. Their dreams of careers on the high seas. The lost loves of girls back home. The fear of death that came from anesthesia. She got them to open up and support each other. They left the hospital with much more than just the losing of their teeth. She had taught them a human moment. They had gained skills they did not know they had.

Our relationship was not an easy one. My defensiveness made me dismissive of her. She would guide me through a case, and I would often disagree with her just to demonstrate how smart I was, and how in control. She would lean in and ask questions about my feelings, which I thought were irrelevant to "the case at hand," which often required my skillful advocacy or bright observation. She was quiet, but firm, with me. She absorbed much that should have angered anyone, but instead kept demanding more from me emotionally. Over the course of the year, she skillfully picked which cases I should work on, each one becoming more and more about the struggles of human relationship and less and less about the quick fixes of hard service delivery.

She had suggested that I had some difficulties "with loss and death," which I quickly denied. "Louise," I said, "I worked four years in an emergency department. I shoveled people out of ambulances, and into hearses. I once scraped a jumper off the street. I have pulled suicides out of closets. I have breathed life in and watched breath leave. Of all the things I know, I know death. Whatever issues I may have, it's not with death. I have eaten death for breakfast."

She had this expression that set my teeth on edge: "I'm kinda wonderin' what you're thinkin'?" My father the grammarian would have washed my mouth out with soap if I'd ever said such a thing. Yet, she used it skillfully and often. Over months and months, she used it on me, and in little baby steps I began to tell her, what I was thinking. Really thinking, and then feeling, and really feeling. She let me have my distance, yet in doing so, I grew close.

I was in the hospital on Mondays, Wednesdays, and Fridays. In the late spring of the year, she set me to work on one "case" that would last for almost five weeks: an old sailor, Mr. Stack, who had been transferred from the VA.[3] He was ventilator dependent but quite conscious and riddled with oat cell cancer. He knew he was going to die eventually, but wanted to get free of the ventilator. He had requested transfer to the Public Health Service hospital, because he said his doctors at the VA didn't want to work on getting him off the machine.

The young internal medicine resident assigned to his case had never weaned anybody off a ventilator. He told me it could be done, but was a little anxious as it was a new procedure for him. The issue, he said, was one of getting the patient stronger, preparing him to use his own respirations, and that the patient had become too panicky when disconnected from the machine in the past.

My first interviews with the patient were pencil and paper affairs, as he could not talk. He made clear he wanted to breathe on his own, but admitted getting scared when disconnected from the respirator—a feeling like drowning. He also felt the resident was scared as well and would "give in" to the patient's panic too early. I noted multiple dates tattooed on his ankle. When I asked about these, he indicated that each date was when, as a merchant mariner during World War II, he'd been on a ship that had been torpedoed at sea. We discussed each date. This was a man who was familiar with the feeling of drowning.

Over the next week or so, we formed a team, we three: the patient, the resident, and I. I suggested we bring in the nutritionist for a consult, as according to the history, the patient had been bed-ridden and not eating for some time and had lost weight. We brought in the physical therapy and respiratory therapy people to help us understand how to help Mr. Stack get stronger. We experimented with exercising the lungs, holding our breath, examining our own "feelings of drowning," and finding ways to both relax and yet hope to restart the process of

Mr. Stack breathing on his own. In the end, we were successful. We had invested in each other and found accomplishment.

Sometime during the night, two weeks after we succeeded in helping Mr. Stack wean from the respirator, the patient disconnected himself from his IV, slipped out onto the sun porch of the hospital, smoked a cigar, cracked open a couple of beers that a buddy must have smuggled in, and washed down a handful of pain pills that he had secretly been storing up. He was found sitting dead facing up at the constellation Gemini: Castor and Pollux, the ancient twin stars protecting sailors.

At the end of the week, I had supervision. Louise always began with an open question, allowing me to take the hour where I wanted. I began like many weeks, giving a rundown of the clients I'd seen, the actions we'd taken, the progress made, the outcomes achieved. As I got to Mr. Stack, I simply reported it like an item from the newspaper. "Mr. Stack was found dead Wednesday night on the 6th sun porch. He had apparently taken an overdose and alcohol. Now, Mrs. Johnson on 4th floor...."

She cut me off. "Wait a second. Mr. Stack, you and Dr. Simmons spent a lot of time with him. I'm kinda wonderin' what you're thinkin'?"

I was going to blow her off. I was going to tell her I didn't think anything. I worked with the patient. I was successful in helping to achieve his goals, and he'd died. That's that. But I couldn't.

I was frozen. I had no words, and inside me my throat was swelling to a painful knot. My mind was an unintelligible maelstrom of pain. I was filled with old stories of loss and grief. I was silent. I was stuck. I could feel time throbbing in my temples, and I was acutely aware that I wanted to fill the silence, but I could not make words come to my shuttered mouth.

She was so good. She sat head down, still and accepting of the silence, until I thought I would burst. She slowly slid her sensibly shoed foot over to mine, and with the touch of her toe upon mine, unlocked me into a release of wrenching sobs. I had not cried in years. The tears burned as they poured through my clenched fists. She reached into my sobs with a question, "What's going on inside you now?"

I surrendered as I had nowhere else to go except into the craziness I was experiencing. I told her about the turtle, the girlfriend, and the sailor. How these crazy things were all swirling together and causing me to cry like a baby. She explored each of them in turn and appreciated the depth of feeling I had given to these moments. She took my pain, made me voice it, and gave validation to the worth that sprang from it. She took my connection and loss to the turtle, the girlfriend, and the sailor and showed me how at the core of this pain was my essential love. How in loving things comes also the pain of loss, but how wonderful to have loved, to be loved, to have the capacity for love. I dried my tears, and knew that my decisions to come to social work were much deeper than I knew, and that I was deeper than I knew.

By the end of the year, I had faced many demons that I had not known dwell within me. Each Friday at 3 o'clock had gone from being a time of defensive dread to being an eager engagement with a caring mother who offered me the moment of emotional rebirth. The stuff of those hours is now often the stuff of the stories I tell my students. It is the stuff of the wonder that is the field experience magic. It is the stuff that social workers do so well. What a gift she gave to me, and she would insist, I to her, in that field year. What a gift that our profession demands that we give this gift to others. The only way to learn social work is by learning with a caring practitioner in the field.

I am lucky to have had Louise. But the name really doesn't matter. Let us each take a moment to think of our own Louises. And give thanks for their lives and skills.

In the end, what I remember about Louise was how large she was. Large in her heart, large in her skills, large in being part of this profession that is larger than us all. In my heart, she is still very much alive.

I can hear her now: "I'm kinda wonderin' what you're thinkin."

9/11 Zen (2001)

It was a clear and crisp October afternoon in northwestern Wisconsin. My kids and the dog were playing in the leaves. Bright orange yellow oak. Raking them into piles and then jumping into them, Scattering them about. Doing it over and over.

We were lying in the leaves, laughing, looking up into the bright blue afternoon.

"Wow!" says Colin. "Lookit that! What is that, dad?!"

"B-52, and escort fighter, off the pilot's left. Way high up. East to west. Almost soundless."

"I never saw that before," says Colin. "Neither have I," says me. "Lets go in and get some cocoa."

Post-Modern Regret

I saw him on a clear autumn morning, watching strong youngsters run cross-country. He had spent much of his life teaching research methods to social work students. The flashing bodies ran by in their various school colors. Crowds cheered them on. I could see the life that was leaving his face. He was ill and would soon die.

"You know," he said, "they really don't care about research. Most people don't even care about facts."

The Speed of Decision: SEPpH

A number of years ago he had killed his entire family. He was in prison for years, mostly in solitary, as they knew he was crazy and couldn't protect himself in the general population. He spent years by himself, except for the company of a colony of ants.

"They were my closest friends," he said.

I met him in a psychiatric hospital where he had finally been transferred. He was a small and skinny sort. And twice a day, I filled a cup with orange juice and more Thorazine syrup than I thought any human being could possibly drink. He would drink it down without batting an eye. He was a gentle man, and I never heard him say anything crazy.

One day on day shift, it was reported that he said he wanted to kill the President of the United States. During the evening shift, two guys from the Secret Service came to interview him. They decided that the hospital was not secure enough, and too close to Washington, D.C. They gave me papers authorizing his release into their authority. I had the charge nurse paged. He came up and reviewed the paperwork. They packed up his few possessions, he waved good-bye to us, and they took him away to a hospital in the Midwest that none of us could find on either a map or in a phone book.

The Looking-Glass Self[4]

"I want to thank you," he said.

"For what?" I asked.

"For calling me by my name," he said.

Two nights before, I had basically kicked him out of the Emergency Room. I spent hours looking for a shelter bed, but there was no room under anybody's roof, and it was cold outside. I'd given him six bus tokens.

"Mr. Washington, I tried. I called every place I can think of, but everybody is full up. I'm afraid you'll have to ride the Number 8. This should get you three loops. I'm really sorry, Mr. Washington, but you can't stay here. Do you know what to do?"

It was the longest route in the metro, it ran all night, and as long as he paid, he wouldn't get kicked off. Three loops would buy him about six hours, time for the places that opened up in the morning breakfast for the homeless.

"Yeah, he said. I'll sit way in the back."

Now he was back at the triage desk asking for "the worker." I smiled and offered my hand. "Hi, Mr. Washington, what can I do for you?"

He said he only used four tokens and he was bringing back the two he hadn't used. I told him to keep them to use how he wished, and how sorry I was still about the other night.

"All day long, people pass me by and they look all around like I'm invisible. Most nights when it gets quiet I tries to make myself invisible, so nobody don't bother me. You do that for so long you don't feel much like a person no more."

"You called me by my name. You can see me."

He smiled, waved good-bye, and walked out the door.

Killing Brendan   (I go, Ego, We go)

He was such a small thing, but he was so loud. He could cry for what seemed like such a long time. He was my first born, and in those first weeks after his birth, we soon grew exhausted from the massive demands he made upon us: feeding, wiping, diapering, holding, consoling, singing, feeding, wiping, diapering, holding, consoling, singing, feeding wiping diapering.

We started sleeping in shifts, as it made no sense that we both should be awake. It was my turn one Sunday afternoon. I had fed, wiped, and diapered, and yet he was still crying. That usually meant it was time for the holding and walking. In motion in his little "papoose" against my chest, I would path a circle in the living room. The rhythm of my steps and the rocking usually lulled him to sleep after some feeding, wiping, diapering. Upon awakening, he was usually good for some moments of alert, but quiet, rocking-walking, followed by some crying that meant more feeding, wiping, diapering.

But today he just seemed inconsolable. No matter what I did, he did not drift off to sleep. I went through my array, praying he would not wake his napping mother upstairs. I paced my circle, watching the Buffalo Bills play football, walking, walking, walking.

I was tired, too, but it was my watch. I tried to feed. He cried. I tried to wipe. He cried. I tried to diaper. He cried. I paced, and rocked and paced and paced some more, and all he did was keep crying. A jagged little wail. A persistent little goat-cry with a red beet face. I tried to distract myself by glancing at the TV, but I had long ago lost track of the score. It was just a shining green point of reference, my mind numb.

He cried some more, and I rocked to no consolation. I paced in hopelessness, and then IT dawned on me how powerless and small he was. It dawned on me how easily I could make him stop.

I had never been to that dark place of horror before. I had never been to that place of such frustration that I could consider smothering the life from another. In an instant, I was rocked in my very being at awareness of the utter violence that I knew now was contained within me. I shuddered as I knew I could be a monster. I quaked as I realized how I could become the instrument of my own son's death. I was filled with shame and horror. I choked with a cloud of guilt and sorrow and self-rage. I was torn in a way that I had never been torn.

As I sank into this blood red-blackness, I was instantly pulled into the consciousness that I also had the power *not* to act.

I was superman against my own darkness. I was the defender against the enemy within. It was a bright and liberating light. I was buoyed in that bleak moment into a place of strength and love. It was a remarkable moment to transform so quickly. To understand the depths of loathing and self accomplishment in so short a time. I became this thing that was so much deeper and wider than I was before. I knew I was now a father. In that moment when I knew I could kill Brendan, and I knew I would not, I became re-born.

He cried, and I paced, and I rocked, and I held him close. We had made each other precious.

DNKA (Did Not Keep Appointment)

Nikky lay down on the railroad track.

He'd run out of trying. He'd run out of money. He'd run out of friends. He'd run out of lines. Whatever had led him to this love affair with the needle had been long forgotten. It didn't matter anymore.

It wasn't a matter of leaving a note. There was nothing to say. He'd been sorry so often there was no forgiveness left in the word.

It was a perfect afternoon to get high. The sunshine was warm, and far above there were light and wispy clouds.

Chestnuts

There are these chestnuts, which we have in social work, that are so cliché, and yet invite us into considerations of great depth. "Begin where the client is," "go with the defense," "content and process," "person in environment," "Beginnings, middles, and ends." There are a good number of others, and we've all heard them often. They easily roll off the tongues of those of us who dwell in this profession of professional "do gooders." They are the headings we find in the opening paragraphs of our textbooks. They are the pithy little comments we throw out as we walk down some busy hall. They serve us in many ways.

They help us signal each other from across the table of interdisciplinary team meetings. They are the secret passwords of our club. They are our wink of recognition. We may come from different agencies, practices, states, or even countries, but as the meeting proceeds, we know who around the table is one of "us." Thus identified, we can begin to engage whatever cause brought us to this meeting, safe in the knowledge that others in the room share our certain understandings. Others share our values. Others share a sense of vision of where this all might go. Together, we will look out upon this table, and together we will begin to "work" it.

These chestnuts help us center ourselves as we begin the difficult work of a helping relationship. Not only cues to outside collaborators, they are often the stuff of the quick and quiet internal dialogues that take place outside of the client's view. Behind our eyes, we remind ourselves and observe ourselves as we observe others. We remember to listen to the words, and also watch the behavior. We remember to listen to the words and watch their effect, on ourselves, on the other, on this relationship. We observe where we are. In the beginning, in the middle, in an end, there are tasks to be engaged. There is a process to follow. We are not lost in what can be a chaotic jungle of life.

They comfort us, these chestnuts, for social work is always about being in the middle. And the middle can be a lonely place to be. We are always guests in another's house. Physicians and nurses live in the hospital. The social worker is the one person in the hospital who brings the "outside in." The social worker is the one most concerned about how patients' lives will be when they go home. A home that is also not ours, but the patients'. The teacher owns the classroom. The social worker in the school knows the demands of children's learning spring well beyond four walls. The social worker is the ambassador of "other," outside the schoolhouse system. The genius of the social worker is that she or he is always between things. The master of the art appreciates the muddle which is life and demands a profession that dances down a razor's edge. But such a place is lonely. There are few who understand this art, the products of which are so freely given away. But the chestnuts can comfort us. In the middle of whatever moment we might be, when they come to our focused mind, we know that they are the words of those who have gone before us. They will be the words of those who will come after. We are never alone with these words with us.

The chestnuts are also seeds. And like seeds, at first they seem so small and simple. And also like seeds, they are the stuff that is so packed with the vitality of our profession. As we take them into ourselves, we are nourished. As we grow in our social work lives, we will come from time to time and reflect upon one of these chestnuts. So simple, at first.

Yet as we ponder more, there is depth and complexity that they reveal. Something as simple as "content and process" enriches our consideration of some boundary we discover somewhere in the world. The admission to the nursing home. The conflict in a foster home. The diagnosis in a clinic. Waves and sand making beaches, ever moving, ever shifting, and yet so there. The chestnuts sometimes clarify our thoughts, and at other times, stretch them into ever more complex places, as a tendril reaches delicately into space.

In this past season of conflict, fear, and anger, I have spent many hours with the weight of one of my chestnuts, "neutrality." As the clouds of war loomed, I concerned myself most with those who would be most vulnerable. Inside my home, and outside on my street, there were often those who grew angry and confused with my position. They sought my company in their marches for, or against. How easy, I thought, it would be to join a side. I would be right, in someone's eyes, no matter which way I turned. But there are beginnings, middles, and ends. And I had to steel myself to provide others shelter from the storm. I focused on how best to be for those caught in the middle, and "did what needs to be done."

How wonderful that we have these chestnuts. A pocketful of them will carry us through the long hike of a social workers' life. When we are confused, they will settle us. When we are hungry, they will nourish us, and make us grow. When we are lonely, we know that we can, and always will, share them.

They are rich and sweet. Have some, won't you?

The Hard Good-bye

He was probably one of the smartest patients I had ever known—a brilliant young man who was extremely well educated. During his exit interview from the psychiatric day hospital, he spent much of the hour telling me how bad his experience had been.

He said that his entire stay since his inpatient hospitalization was a waste of the four months he had spent coming to the center. The other patients were losers. The staff was incompetent. The psychiatrist was an ignoramus. And I, the center director, was a fraud. He was going back gratefully to his original psychiatrist, who was a brilliant man who had unfortunately been duped by all of us. He could hardly wait for his next appointment so that he could tell him what a sham the day program had been.

As he walked down the hallway to the exit, he yelled profanities at all the staff. Their mouths dropped. "Adios, Motherf***ers!" he yelled, as he slammed the door.

Everybody was shaking their heads as they peeked into my office. "Well, that didn't go well." "What did we do wrong?" "What a shame." The comments reflected a sense of failure and self-blame, or blame on the patient.

"Hold on, everybody," I said. "Let's look at the care plan: Goal 1—stabilize gains; post-hospitalization acute psychosis with personality disorder—So, medication adherence, good. Labs within therapeutic limits, good. Symptoms stable, no psychosis, so, 'Check.' Goal 2—Explore and secure stable living situation—three and a half months in same apartment with stable roommate, 'check.' Goal 3—Explore and secure steady part-time employment—working three days a week at public library, 'check.' Goal 4—return part-time to school—enrolled in two college courses, satisfied with mid-term grades, registered for subsequent semester, again, 'check.'"

"Folks, this is a successful case. Every goal accomplished or well under way. I feel very good about him. He's back in the care of his referring doc. He's accomplished all that he set out to do since he got out of the hospital. Some people just have a hard time saying good-bye. His way is 'Adios, Motherf***ers.' That's the way it is with some folks."

As far as I know, he did okay.

The Dead Man

I escorted them up from the E.R. to the surgical ICU. Out of the darkness, with a single light above the bed, he lay Christ-like in reverse Trendelenberg.[5] A big man, his body was muscular, ebony, shiny, and except for the 4x4 over his right eye, perfect. His size had probably been his undoing. He'd been a defensive end at Coppin for two years until his grades went south and he dropped out of football to join the game on the street. He didn't do drugs, his mother told me, but he did sell them.

Trapped in the long narrow barroom by two of the city's finest, he did what only came natural; he rushed them looking for a way out. A smaller man would have been wrestled to the ground. His speed and his size were threatening, and one of the cops sent a bullet across his brain. Three blocks from the E.R., the paramedics played swoop and scoop and we didn't pronounce him. We kept his body alive and packaged him for the surgical ICU. The cops had called the family who were on the way. The attending asked me to call the organ procurement organization (OPO). I told them the situation and they put their social worker in a car.

"He looks so beautiful, at peace," his mother said, "yet he seems so alive." A small tear escaped from the side of her eye. She stared straight ahead at her once vibrant son, his lungs triggering a respirator, the world dark and silent except for the hums and small sounds of the machines, his powerful chest rising and falling.

"His body is being kept oxygenated by the respirator, Mrs. Jefferson," the worker from the transplant agency said quietly, but in a careful matter-of-fact tone. "But he's no longer alive. His brain has gone and it's just the machines right now."

I had worked with my colleague from the organ procurement organization before. While I tended to be solicitous in death with family members, she was very careful and direct. Her language quite chosen and sometimes, I thought, a little terse.

Down in the E.R., I'd met with the family and the attending physician who notified that their son had died. By prior arrangement, my role was to indicate to the family that because of his strong and young body, and the fact that he'd been killed from a gunshot, he'd been placed on a respirator until the family had seen him and discussed whether he could be considered for organ donation. Physicians declared death; the social worker broached organ donation. The OPO worker explained the donation process. Now here in the ICU, I could tell that the dead man's mother was struggling to believe her son was dead, and struggling to make a decision concerning her son's body.

We talked about her son. She was angry. She was sad. She was guilty. She was disbelieving. She grieved quietly at the bedside. I asked her if I could help her make any phone calls. Was there anyone else who could help make arrangements? She smiled and shook her head. She mentioned the name of an undertaker in the neighborhood that she would call. The OPO worker quietly asked if she could help in any way. Mrs. Jefferson sighed and nodded.

"He was a good boy, but he'd done some bad things." She looked over at the OPO worker. "Maybe from this bad thing some good can come. Just give him back to me when it's all over." We sat for a little more until she asked when he was going to the OR. "Soon." I said.

She rose and kissed him good-bye and said she wanted to leave. I escorted her and her friend to the door of the E.R. and walked out onto a warm night on Monument Street. I gave her my card with all the other paperwork and told her to call me if there was anything else. "It was a sad time and I was sure there were things that were left unsaid, and things unthought-of, if we can be of any help, please call."

She shook my hand. "Thank you for taking care of my baby."

I walked inside to see if there was anything else to do with the OPO worker. My shift had an hour left. I hoped I could get the paperwork done, so I could go home and hug my kids.

Decathexis[6]

They loved her so very much, and she loved them. Some had come from thousands of miles away. Throughout the weekend, they had kept a vigil, reading to her from a family bible, holding her tiny hand, stroking her hair. She would slip in and out of consciousness, but upon awakening, always slowly look about and smile. Her breathing was shallow and labored. They offered her fluids, but she would often just silently refuse.

She beckoned me closer.

"Need...t'be...alone." She whispered.

"I understand, Anna. Good-bye." I whispered into her ear.

I asked the family if they would follow me into the hallway, closing her door. I explained to them that the patient loved them all very much, but she told me she needed a moment to herself. I asked if they would like to take a moment down the hall in the chapel, and they agreed.

She only needed five minutes and was gone.

Becoming Full

Earlier this year, without much fanfare, in a white number 10 business envelope, I received a simple letter from my Chancellor promoting me to Full Professor. The brief text informed me of a modest raise in salary and an expression of appreciation for my services to the university. It was impossible not to take stock for a moment. A little over a decade has passed since I came to this little Lake Wobegon of a college town to teach undergraduates. Coming to academic life was a second career, and a considered choice on how to raise a family. How quickly both have grown, I thought. No longer an apprentice. No longer a journeyman. They had given me the master's papers, as my oldest began packing for college. I was not sure what to do next.

I have lived 50+ years. I looked out my office window and considered men of action and men of words. I had reached that age, where I sense the tipping point in my life, where I feel like I've become more of the latter than the former. In a year when there were so many demands for action, the world outside me asked me to contribute words.

I encouraged a colleague and friend, recently back from working a combat stress company in the "sandbox," to visit my young students and lecture on his experience. He talked of the importance of letting soldiers tell their stories. I encouraged him to tell his. He made the fundamentals of social work shine in a different, brutal new light. I moderated the conversation between students and soldier social worker. As low autumn afternoon sunlight found its way into the auditorium, I knew sometimes he was looking onto the desert. The young women in the front row were looking into themselves, finding the things discussed in classroom connected to something deeper than they had previously thought. I could see some looking for a courage that they hoped yet to discover. I considered men of action and words. I felt "professorial" in that I had arranged the soldier and the students to come together, but I was jealous of my friend's experience.

With the end of last summer, as yet more waters flushed through the Gulf States, I spent evenings working for the feds doing what the professorship has trained in me well: grading papers.

I reviewed applications for the federal disaster crisis counseling programs generated in the aftermath of the gulf storms. I provided advice on sheltering and health care programs. Hundreds of thousands had been dislocated across the country. In between my classes, I sat in telephone conferences discussing the pros and cons of spending tens of millions of dollars. I would offer words about directions and misdirections the government would make. I would be thanked by some hurried official; someone would tell me a check was in the mail, and then I would hang up the phone.

On the path to my next lecture, sometimes I would sit down and look about me. Scrubbed faces with backpacks were smiling and chatting and walking to and from lectures. They and I were safe and secure. We would talk about the diaspora from a distance. Some of them would pick up, and go south, and hang sheet rock. It was difficult for me not to feel absurd.

For completely different reasons, I would take planes out east and sit in meetings on odd weekends in Washington. Again, "grading papers" or participating in the giving of opinion. Between the conferences, or at cocktails, my colleagues at the Red Cross would be discussing recent missions to Sri Lanka, Pakistan, or Geneva. They would drop that they had seen so and so, who had been in India but had been seconded to Darfur. They themselves were glad to be finished with their work in Aceh, but eager to get on to the Sahel. They were polite when they inquired after my family in Wisconsin. They were people of action, again, and I was a user of words.

Outside the window, the students are loading their belongings into cars and trucks. For some it will be a summer away from study; for others it will be the beginning of their lives in action. The graduation parties are past celebrations. The commencement has been walked. The pomp and circumstance has been. It will get quiet here in this little upper Midwestern town. I will clean up the debris from desk, and floor, and any other horizontal space in this clutter of an office. So much paper. So many words.

St. Thomas Aquinas[7] just became silent one day. His ineffability arose from some great insight that rendered all his words into chaff. He made no more. It was, he said, "all straw." I have had no blinding enlightenments, but wonder if I have become too full of words, and have starved for action. If this is the crisis of mid-life, it will not solve with sports cars or foolish romantic entanglements. In becoming the "Full Professor," I have become lost as to where to go. I wonder if I have been at this for too long.

Still staring out the window, self absorbed, and self conscious of the selfishness of my own pity, I was interrupted by the phone. It was Kara, who had graduated two years ago. "Dr. Rogers, "she said, "I've called to tell you I'm eating my words."

I was puzzled and struggled with my memory. I remembered her as earnest, but cantankerous and quarrelsome over the senior year and her Baccalaureate thesis. She had hated doing it, and hated me for mentoring her through it. Many moments had been spent arguing to me how inane the exercise was. How the research effort was not the heart of social work. How it was just months making words that only one little man would read. She had written about incarcerated women and their communication with their children. It was, in the end, as I remember, a modest and half-hearted final effort, but respectable enough for a "B." I never expected to hear from her again.

"I wanted to let you know that I got my dream job, and I've been doing it for six months." She started somewhat tentatively. "I'm working with incarcerated moms and their families. I'm supervising a program that is helping to strengthen their connections. I facilitate visits. I help bridge bars. I never felt more alive, and I'm doing good work." I was polite and happy for her, over the phone, still not sure as to the point of the call.

"I wanted to let you know how sorry I am for giving you so much trouble about the thesis a few years ago." She continued, more forthrightly. "I showed the DOC my thesis when I interviewed for a position, and the people there were so impressed, they hired me into a position I hadn't even applied for. It's my dream job. It's really important work."

I took a moment and congratulated her, and was offering her good wishes when she interrupted me.

"It wasn't just words, Dr. Rogers," she said. "I need to thank you for struggling with me about the thesis. The words got me the job. The words put me into the middle. The words were—the words are—real social work. You helped me find them, and I put them into action. I can't thank you enough, and I kinda know that my moms thank you, too. I just had to call and say that."

I accepted her gift. We chatted a little small talk more, and then we each rang off.

Looking out the window again, watching the students leaving, I was no longer feeling pathetic. I could not say that the vision of the future was any clearer, but I discarded like chaff any conflict between words and action. I was becoming full, and it was good to become full.

Olfaction

She was only in my office for a few minutes. A wet November snow was melting on her coat as she asked me a few questions about some courses she thought she was supposed to take, a freshman. She was up and out after a few short answers and on her way down the hall.

I couldn't figure out why I had such a powerful affinity for her. I instantly liked her. I hardly even knew her. She was a student. She wasn't a pretty girl. Yet, I was flushed with feelings that I knew I had to conceal and control. I was, after all, 30 years her senior and a professor.

Then it dawned on me. She smelled of wet wool.

Some thirty years earlier, on a cold wet November night, I walked down Connecticut Avenue with a woman her age, just a few blocks from the Chevy Chase Circle. We were walking her family's dogs, as an excuse to be out from under their roof and be alone together. Both freshmen at different colleges, we used the Thanksgiving break to re-kindle an adolescent summer romance. I wore a too-large stadium coat bought at a second-hand store. She wore a Navy pea-coat. I had forgotten gloves and she had lent me a spare of knitted mittens. We held hands. The wet falling snow was too fragile in the not yet frozen night, and it melted on the wool. I am sure in the street light I caught a wisp of steam rising from her shoulders.

I will never forget that aroma.

A Scary Story

Dear All on Socwork: (A Listserv on the Internet)

Recently, Bart wrote: I don't remember anyone suggesting that most rich people like to watch poor people starve. I doubt that many would consider this as entertaining as counting their money.

As long as there is a nice campfire started (Tim puts out fuel, real wood; Matthew just throws gasoline all about), I think I'll pull up a stool, put on my cubmaster's broad brimmed campaign hat, set down a cuppa joe, and tell you a little story on this fine starlit night. (Yes, little Stevie, you can whittle with your new penknife...just don't throw the shavings into the fire.)

It was on just such a night like this. I was around another campfire. The stars were blazing, and, every so often, one of the Perseids meteors would briefly punch the atmosphere with a bright cosmic firework. Just like tonight, we'd all go "ooohh" for a moment. But, the campfire I was around then was almost 10 years ago, and it wasn't here in socworkspace, it was in the "real" world. (Matthew, you like "real," don't yew...I always see you telling the other little cubbies what "real" is...that's helpful of you son...be careful with that gasoline! A little goes a long way!)

Well now, where was I? Oh, yes. This campfire I was tellin' you all about was in the "real" world. A place called "The Hamptons." It was a nice campfire. On the beach. The stars above just a'blazin, and the sound of the surf had been joinin' with the chilled white wine to lull all around the fire into a cozy blissful feeling. ("Man, it don't get no better'n this.") There were four of us: an old fraternity buddy of mine, a traveler of many road trips with me who now was an up&comer in the same multinational his dad had worked; my wife, the rock who always gave me safe harbor when I had ventured into the dark side; me, a psychic traveler who had settled into running a detox and psychiatric service on a tattered side of a faraway city; and, lets call her "Melanie," my buddy's new bride of a year.

High above us, beyond the dunes, was Melanie's daddy's house. It had about 10 bedrooms. We'd all spent the weekend there, riding horses, playin' tennis, drinkin' a lot. ("Now you boyz remember this is a 'big people's' story...cubbies don't drink!") Actually, it wasn't "really" Melanie's Daddy's house. It was just his "cottage." The "real" houses were in Upstate, and Colorado, and Geneva ("that's in Switzerland, Marie").

Anyways, after a wonderful couple of days, we were now settin' around this fire on the beach. We'd eaten clams and lobsters, and drank cold, cold, Chablis. It was gettin' to that time that the conversation around a campfire gets to what I call "truth tellin' " (which most often is just "lie-tellin' " in the face of cosmic ambiguities that seem too big to comprehend, but it makes us all feel like we're doin' sumphin'!). Well, boys and girls, the conversation got around to the troubles of the world. I think we was gettin' pretty narrowly focused on the costs, benefits, and troubles of public education in a democracy when me and Melanie started to get square in opposite corners (she was so beautiful, so willowy; she was so rich—what did she possibly see in my buddy?). I was trying to explain to her why it was necessary for the wealthy, "the village," to share more of it, or else one day people might rise up and violently take crazy matters into crazy hands. I went into this long and righteous argument that came outta many years of sittin' in social policy classes and "the front lines." Wellsir, let me tell ya, I think I finished my soliloquy with sumphin' that went like: "Melanie, what are you going to do when 'they' come rushin' outta cities and start smashing up you'alls little cottages?"

Well, let me tell you sumphin'. I had not put the question mark on my sentence when this beautiful, genteel woman looked at me without a hint of worry in her brow, with all the confidence of a steel blade sheathed in velvet, and she said: "They've got to get over the bridges, and they're easy to blow up. They've got to get over eight lanes of beltway, and it's an easy target to lay fire over such a broad plain. The poor will always prefer oppression and order and a small crumb over their own anarchy anyway. Middle classes come and go, and I can get on a plane and go anywhere worth going in the world, anytime I want."

Well, boys and girls, I took a big slurp of my wine and looked out onto the night surf. I had no words. The conversation switched to lighter things, like travel and such. In the back of my mind, I wrote off her blithe attack to just the posturings of two people who cared for the same man in different parts of his history, fueled by sun and sand and Chablis.

But I think she meant what she said. And I'll never forget it.

Well now, that's my little campfire story. It's just an anecdote about one little rich girl. The scientist in me would never generalize it to other folk.

And the cubmaster in me just thought since we had a little flame goin' on here anyway, I might as well roast an old story on it. Well now cubs, I think it's time for bed. Bart, the latrine's thataway. You take Jeff and a flashlight. Tim, you're the oldest here, so set an example for the others. And Matthew, if your bunk's been short-sheeted again, don't come whinin' that the other boys did it.

There's a rich girl out in the woods somewhere. I can just feel it in the wind.

County Fair: The End of Summer

I am sitting on a bench at the Pierce County Fair. A slow wind from the south has made it humid for western Wisconsin, and in the late late afternoon, the elm that shades me is welcome. I am waiting for my wife, the quilter. She, from "out East" and her big city ways, will soon stroll down this little midway with this smug little smile on her face and a grand champion ribbon on this year's project. She's taken top prizes two years in a row and secretly enjoys beating the "locals" on their own turf.

But I am not focused on the strengths or weaknesses of my wife's competitive streak. Facing a new school year, where I teach social work at the local university, I am enveloped in the deep sensuality of August—a month, which for me has always been filled deeply with the ambivalences of life. Innocence mingles with the sinister; good dances with evil. There is an awareness that the lush of midsummer is at end, and the ending of summer things comes nigh.

The midway is awash in the paradox of the lengthening shadow of late summer sun. In August, everything living knows that death approaches. In that awareness, the drama of opposites plays itself out at the county fair. Yellow jackets become more aggressive in their struggle for my bratwurst and beer. They will soon die, and they seek to eat much of life before it's over. The black-eyed Susan is its most yellow. The music of the carousel is loud in the anticipation of winter's silence. Usually careful Harrys eat fried food under the VFW tent. Food rich with grease rolls slowly over tongues that will eat potatoes and canned green beans all winter long. The air is filled with deep perfumes of popcorn, sweat, and patchouli. I smell sex with just the slightest touch of the sinister all about.

Milk maidens, all of 15 years, parade their 4H heifers in the afternoon, their cows and themselves clean scrubbed to a pink blush on the cheek. The beef judges only see the bright young innocence of Lutheran Sunday schoolers. As the evening approaches, however, t-shirts are knotted into halters that unveil nubile tummies, the occasional navel ring. Hidden cachés of eye makeup and lip rouge emerge from pockets to paint a lusty pout on a face that could melt a celibate. They rove in small bands and flirt with the tattooed carny boys, sinister boys from far away who smell of marijuana and beer. Glances are inflamed on Ferris wheels. Sometimes they walk as a pair. I spy one young woman-girl walking too closely with the summer boyfriend, a soft youth who is just beginning to show the stretch of adulthood.

He seems so clueless when she says, "Do you want to go see the water treatment plant?"

"Uh sure, okay...but why?" says he, counting his change and deciding if he can play more ski-ball. She tugs at his arm in a manner that is playful and yet urgent. There is a mystery to be revealed. He will never know what hit him.

Soon it will be time for the pattern of the school year. Expected. Predictable. The students will come, lectures will be given, books read, and tests taken. The thing I try to teach, social work, is well reminded by the county fair. The serendipity that emerges when yin meets yang. The humanity that struggles with love and lust, dreams and schemes drenched in deep aromas of too much perfume and popcorn. The books and outlines are ordered and follow a logic and a rhythm that is expected for both student and professor. But who really is the recipient of the social work I teach? Is it not these yellow jacket human beings who pray to be "good" and yet flit fiercely in lights that go astray? Is it not from the life, yearning in the pressured kiss of a young couple soon to be separated by September, that our profession draws its strength? Walt Whitman's "yawp!" was meant for August nights in the carnival lights of the Midway. The clown face on the carny wagon is both loving and tragic, evil and good, vulnerable and yet strong. August is a Trickster's month, and tricksters drank deep of life by skating down the razor's edge of what is ideal and real, what is loving and hateful. Lucifer was the angel who knew God best.

A wasp circles my beer and ultimately stings me on the back of my palm. A backwards swat makes his last act of aggression his oblivion. Yet his kiss alerts and alarms me. His death has made me more alive. In a day and age when so many seek such clear black and white lines, I am impassioned by this August dance of death and life—the playfulness that boundaries have of each other.

People have so much because they face so little. A social worker is well reminded of the urgencies that play themselves out on the August Midway—that people are in that space "in between." Above the carnival lights grows the deep black of the August night. Here in the midway, we will find human beings. We would do well to dance with them the dance of life. The tears and the smiles will become the stuff of stars falling in the sky.

Nice Work, If You Can Get It

There were still 10 minutes left in the hour when, apparently satisfied, smiling, she gathered her things and stood, extending her hand.

"Thank you, this has been very helpful. I very much appreciate your time and efforts."

I rose, and began returning the grasp of her extended hand. After my initial engagement, she'd launched right in and started telling me about the problems she was having in her marriage. She talked pretty non-stop except for the occasional clarifying question on my part. I hadn't even begun to conceptualize the difficulties in her marriage.

"We have a little time left," I said. "We hadn't really got to talking about where you would like to go from here."

"I'm going home," she said. "I really don't think I need any more of your time, seriously. You've been very helpful. I've had all this stuff bottled up inside for so long that I thought I was going crazy. But now, really, just talking out loud to you about it, I realize it's not as bad as I thought. I feel like I can work this out with Tim. I just needed to get it out and have somebody listen. I don't think I need another session, but if I do, I will set up another appointment."

I finished the handshake and smiled. "Well, I'm glad this was useful for you. I hope things get better for you. I'd appreciate if you would give me a call or drop me a message down the road if you can and tell me how things turn out for you and your husband."

She did, some months later. Whatever it was, they had worked it out.

Post-Traumatic Raison d'etre

Marie had been driving the bus down Pratt Street. Some guy in a Lexus in way too much of a hurry to get back to D.C. wasn't paying attention and t-boned the thing at South Greene Street doing about 40. Most everybody agreed the bus had the light, and the guy in the Lexus was lucky he was just around the corner from the University Hospital E.R.

But the suits who ran the MTA just didn't get it. They were worried about the liability and were gonna assume the operator was at fault until proven otherwise.

So, instead of being nice to Marie, they made her feel like a criminal.

When the Lexus hit the bus, she felt the jolt. She threw on the break, spun in her seat, and scanned the passengers. Little inside the bus was disturbed. Nobody was seated in the one seat where a window had popped in. People looked scared but none the worse for wear. She spun the other way and looked down over the Lexus. It was clear that she better radio for an ambulance at her location. She told everybody on the bus just to remain seated, and flew out of the bus to give the guy in the Lexus first aid. She wasn't worried about liability.

The paramedics took care of the guy. Nobody took care of Marie.

It would have been so simple. All somebody had to do was be nice to her, perhaps offer a sincere note of sympathy, a lift home, a day or two off to mend, a little "we're so sorry this happened to you."

Instead, somebody at headquarters was worried about liability. They wanted reports filled out. They wanted her interrogated. They wanted statements from all the passengers. They wanted a sample of blood and urine for drug testing. They wanted her to blow into a tube to see if she had been drinking.

She noticed it the next morning, a tingling in her hands and feet. It grew into an anxious feeling, and then a fear. She was afraid to walk out of her house. She was afraid to drive a bus. Her lips tingled, too.

She called her family doctor, who saw her, worked her up and down, and could find no physical abnormalities. She was consumed in fear. Now she couldn't sleep and she was losing weight. Her body hurt all over.

She told me that she worried that she would never be able to drive a bus again. She applied for disability. The company fought her. She knew what she felt. It wasn't "in her head." She was depressed and anxious. She hurt. She was hurt. The company would not believe her, and for the next year and a half, she would see me weekly and protest the reality of her experience. I would observe how angry she was, and she would shake it off. She was sick, she would say, and she needed somebody to believe her. I told her I did. She said that wasn't enough.

She would never drive a bus again. She would spend the next two years careening back and forth between doctors, and lawyers and therapists. Many X-rays, depositions, specimens, lawsuits, prescriptions, and witnesses later, by God, they would believe her. The company would give up and settle. She was disabled, they finally said. They would send her checks.

The guy who hit the bus was treated and released the same day, two years earlier. He never sued the MTA, and he never hit another bus.

Marie never drove a bus again. She had no more battles to fight. She got a check every month for her disability. After she cashed the fifth one, she bought a gun and killed herself. She ceased to be a liability.

The Tipping Point
(or, "there she goes again...")

It always happens sometime in August. I'm never quite sure when, or what the moment is.

Perhaps it's the day I notice that all the nestlings from the swallow house have departed—only a curious finch peeking in to see if there is any food left within. Perhaps it occurs in the moment when the tomatoes have gone one day too long and begin to split, or the first geese head in formation south, or the Perseids flash across the night sky. It always happens in August.

There is this tipping point when the lush growth of summer stops, and things slip into harvest. The progress since birth zeniths, the autumn approaches, an element of death enters into the full lushness of growing life.

As a child, I never noticed the nights in August growing shorter. On Marmon Avenue, a block off of Liberty Heights, it was warm and summer dusk for what seemed forever to us, weaving our bicycles through the alleyways. Now in my fifties, and living in the upper Midwest, with its short summers and long winters, the moment when it all changes is more vivid in my consciousness.

And my reaction to the tipping point is always the same.

In the face of the awareness of life's boundaries, I am soon filled with blossoms of my favorite drug, nostalgia. It "pulses through my veins, chasing down the lanes," just like heroin. But this nostalgia is anesthetic in a different way. As I begin to clear the yellowed leaves, as I prepare spaces to put away the lawn furniture, as I tune the snowblower, I am filled with images of my young life. I tend not to feel the rake in my hand, but the intrusion of a memory riding through the Hagerstown Fair in the back seat of a Volkswagen with an 18-year-old woman on my lap and a bottle of Mateus at my side. As I place the wrench on the oil tap, I don't feel my older legs strain in my squat; I am captured of a memory of my young wife and infant son across the aisle of the light-rail train. We are going to get my diploma. Every evening as

228 Beginnings, Middles, & Ends: Sideways Stories on the Art & Soul of Social Work

the sun goes down, from behind my iced tea, I am visited by the ghosts of my youth. They are friendly ghosts and they come swirling with a narcotic of rich emotions, a sweet melancholy of "good ol' times." I see Linda, the girl I danced the twist with in 2nd grade. I am playing electric football with Simeon, listening to *The White Album*. I see Synder, glistening in the May sunshine, leaping for a frisbee as the ice melts on green pony bottles in the beer case. I see Carol bathed in street light from a corner of the North Haven green. It's easy to become drunk on such fare. My wife will come out onto the porch and say, "Where are you?" I must bring my attention from such a long place away.

I've been on the couch long enough to know from whence this sweet defense springs. But like most good neuroses, such insight does not prevent the annual reoccurrence. It does, however, prevent me from enjoying it for too long.

Nostalgia dissolves in a few weeks' time to an awareness that summer is over and it is time for the school year to begin. Here, as I start to see the threads of winter, I need to prepare to engage the fresh faces of students who will come. I feel acutely all my years, and wonder if I have enough inside me, to with them, engage. I feel the dread of the death that is within me.

I remember two comments from people I trusted at Maryland, when I told them I was moving to River Falls to join a BSW program. "Don't get trapped on an island," my mentor said, and, "It's cold up there." A very solid colleague, walking the Inner Harbor with me on the way to commencement, said, "It's better to be a big fish in a small pond, than a bootlicker here the rest of your life," and, "It's cold up there."

All of this, some 15 years later, is quite true. I've grown to be a recognized voice around the table of the university. I've seen enough chancellors come and go that I've become accustomed to the limits of their authority. I've been through enough strategic plans that I know when not to sweat the small stuff. People nod when I pass on the mall.

I've also watched younger, hotter colleagues shine brighter in the hallways of my profession. I've not produced the pages of citations on my C.V. I've been a yeoman, year in and out, setting forward the conditions for 25 young women and (usually) one guy to join the club of do-gooders four years later. I have not lit the world with my scholarship. It seems I'm not destined to live in the Category I. I guess I'm a II-B or not II-B. It's no longer a question.

It's true. It gets cold up here.

So, I get to feeling like a yellowed leaf, and wonder how I will "do it again." And then, that's when it happens, the second phase. The nepenth of nostalgia is replaced by an amphetamine of anticipation. I notice the yellow jackets become more aggressive in those late August picnics.

They take more risk in hopes to get a bite of a burger or a beer. So, too, my mind begins to race as I consider my courses for the fall and I do not fall easily asleep each night. What lecture fell flat last year? What assignment was tiresome? Where was it hard to make the point? What was that cool article I read a couple months ago? How can I change things to make this social work less "education" and more "adventure"?

I will sneak into the office and start to brush up the preps. I will rip stuff out of syllabi and discard it on the floor. I consider a new assignment that I thought of before and never used. I bite my lip and discard an old anchor text and order a new one. All of my attention to the past fades away, and I start to only consider the future. New faces. Old ones scrubbed into a new academic year's demands. Freshmen will be sophomores. Sophomores will be juniors. I wonder how they will have changed. I fantasize the unknown. My heart races. I become excited about the prospects. A mania of possibility takes hold. I am anxious, but it feels good.

And so it is. Harvest is death that begets new life. From what was grown we make nourishment. The ends will post new beginnings. In August, a knowing chill will come someday. I must burn brighter now. I must remake what I've done in the past to remake the future. I must make my well known bright and novel and taste new. That is the stuff of starting again.

A Dog's Life

Here's what it says on yesterday's bill from the veterinarian:

Pt.: Cheddar 15 y.o. mx

Item#	Service	Unit	Price
PS004	Examination -medical problem	$56.50	$56.50
LACC	Blood Chem Profile & CBC	$109.90	$109.90
LAURIA	Urinalysis, Add-on	$27.80	$27.80
RA001	Radiograph- Single view & Interpretation	$53.90	$107.80
EU001	Euthanasia, Cremation no ashes returned	$105.38	$105.38

It only took the X-ray. I looked at the films. I made the diagnosis before the vet did. I saw the massively enlarged heart. I now understood what was in the distended belly. I understood the increased ataxia. I understood why he couldn't move his bowels, was off his food, would take no water that morning. "He's got massive congestive heart failure." The vet said, "That's right—now we don't know why..." I cut her off. "It doesn't matter."

I made the decision. I gave him a little bit of bologna. I said goodbye.

I knew when I saw him go slack he was gone. He breathed agonally, and the vet and tech scrambled for more medicine. I just pressed on his chest and said, "I know what this is, just listen for heart sounds." The vet said, "He's gone."

I said, "Thank you," and left.

Today, I weep.

I've got 27 methodology papers to read and grade for my research class. Thank god it's gray outside. I couldn't stand a sunny day. I understand a little bit more about professional boundaries. I close my office door.

Attachment. It's a bitch. Good-bye buddy. OK, now let's look at Lisa's social policy paper.

Private Troubles, Public Concerns

In the winter of my father's life, we were sitting on the porch looking out over the yard.

"Ya know," he said, "I spent my entire life praying for peace for your generation, and I think it was a mistake."

I, who once carried a draft card and had missed the war in Vietnam by the sheer luck of age, turned square onto him. "I think that's the craziest thing I've ever heard you say!"

"Don't get me wrong. I think war is the most horrible of things. But those of my generation who lived, had the experience of being part of a noble collective effort. We understand that we are the government. We understand that it's important to stand together for a common good. I look at your generation, not you mind you, but your generation. It's all this 'individual freedom to be' nonsense. Freedom is fine, but it's nothing without 'We, The people.'"

I had no evidence, nor heart, to refute him.

The Listener's Tale

The listener sat down in the sand, and for a long while, he stared at the sea. In the darkness, the limits of his vision narrowed his sight to the breaking of the waves on the beach in front of him, the water filled with small particles of phosphorescence. To his left or right, they broke quickly into the black. Over him broke only the endless song of the ocean and the warm, moist summer wind.

He considered the tale told to him by the woman-girl. In his mind's eye, he looked into her mirror and considered the pain. He thought of the laughter turned into tears and confusion. He pondered the wound that wound between the daughter and the man; the love in their darkness. He turned all the thoughts over and over again, even as the waves turned over into the sand.

Wordlessly, he reached into his bag and sought the balm that had brought him to the shoreline. He repeated the tale, as best he could, to the white dove he had carried to this place. He stroked the bird's head and smiled softly. Opening his hands, he released her into the sky. The dove circled briefly above the small, endless sparks of green tumbling in the breakers, and then rose into the night.

The listener lingered with the sea for a few moments more, and then walked to return another night.

Luncheons in May

There was the usual terrible crush at the end of a semester. I promise myself every year that I will not allow it, and every year it returns. There are many papers to read; exams to write, administer, and grade. With all the other odds and ends that press in a day, I always seem to go through this period of two weeks or so, when I become quick, a little testy, and a tad authoritarian. I have so many things to do, and so much on my mind and calendar, that I tend to lose track of things—committee meeting times, car keys, and the odd form that's usually important.

Into this tunnel I had penciled in "Fieldwork supervisors/grad luncheon." It popped out of my calendar book (an item that also usually gets lost this time of year). I rushed over to some room off the commons to attend. Yet another damn thing to do. Papers on my desk were calling.

Lunch was nothing special—soup and sandwich. Yet, after my forced social smile relaxed, I had the chance to look about me. It was a spring sunshine that lit up faces now scrubbed and proud, perched upon straight shoulders and not-quite-but-almost-adult dresses. There were fresh corsages. And to the left of each, a "supervisor." A volunteer/mentor/teacher/demander/supporter who now, in just a few months' time, would be a "colleague." They, too, looked scrubbed and proud.

We all took a little time to eat and "talk shop"—the real work of social work in a university lunchroom. Divisions of ivory tower, student, professor, "field instructor" melting away in a ritual of all "talking shop." All of us colleagues, all of us concerned. As I looked about, I felt some bit of pride in the accomplishments of students who would soon graduate—and of field instructors who had "done good."

I was reminded of a photograph taken in the 1930s of the Residents' Dining Hall at Hull House. Around three tables sit people talking shop, sharing soup. Miss Jane Addams sits at right in the picture. She has a glass of water in her right hand, a linen in her left, and a quiet, and pensive look upon her face. It is difficult to tell if she is focusing on the conversation to her left, or gazing about the room in thoughtful comprehension.

I celebrated that luncheon the other day. I thought about all the other luncheons, in all the other rooms, in all the other years. I celebrated the spirit that brings bridges across generations. That brings care to this moment. I let go of all that end-of-semester pressure nonsense. I reflected, instead, on the passing of this craft and concern, one by one, from older colleague to younger. I celebrated these "people of the middles" who do each day the little possibilities in a profession of the impossible. I sat in quiet comprehension of this thing we call "social work."

This cause, and function.

Note: This story is reproduced with permission from The New Social Worker, Spring 1996, Volume 3, Number 1.

Between Bright Lines, Beliefs, and Bell Curves: The Burden of the Middleweight

Today, we come together to break bread in celebration of your accomplishment of your degree in social work.

Those about the room with more experience are proud of you for your achievement. Secretly, they also harbor a small sense of relief for what you also represent. They are glad that you will soon graduate and join us in the effort we call social work. You are reinforcements in struggle to do good in the world.

Soon you will help us carry what I call the burden of the "Middleweight." It is the hard task of seeing the world in the way we social workers do. It is part of that understanding that I call "getting it."

Three kinds of knowing occupy the consciousness of most of the people you will meet and serve.

On one horizon is the epistemology of Law: What is right or wrong, good or bad, valued or valueless arises ultimately to a forced choice bounded in the history of previous choices, or forged in some battle of a legislature. The lawyers among us strive for what they call "bright lines," that boundary, clearly marked, where one either does, or does not, do. They seek no in-between.

On another horizon, there's the epistemology of science. Set against the assumption of probability, it busies its adherents in the search of what they call empirical truth. They are endlessly generating guesses about the way the world works, driven by the latest set of things they call "facts"—agreements where they have ceased to look any closer, until one of them does, and discovering yet more anomaly, which sets off more rounds of induction, deduction, thesis, and antithesis. Many useful things are gained in this way, but sometimes it is merely an illusion of technique.

And yet still, we will meet those who dwell in the realm of knowing from rich personal and cultural meaning—an anthropological consciousness of symbols and personal attachment brought to us by post-modernists, existentialists, and theologians. Here we will meet people who know what they know grounded in what we might call "Belief." They do bother with bright lines if they do not synch with their dogma. They disregard any of the theories of science, if they do not support the importance of their myth. Their belief is the correct one, even if others disagree.

Some of the trouble in the world comes when the people who occupy one way of knowing collide with persons who think with another. Sometimes trouble occurs when they reach the horizon of their way of knowing, and find their epistemology unable to answer some deep need, and they enter an experience of dread and depression. At the edges of each of these different worldviews are the cracks in which people fall.

And thus, somewhere between Belief, Bright Lines, and Bell Curves is the burden of the Middleweight. The social worker knows that each way of knowing has its own incompleteness. The most perfect Ideal is not universally shared. And reality, when looked upon too closely, is not real.

And so we are faced with doing our impossible tasks. We serve both society and the individual—both units of consciousness in tremendous flux, ever changing, agreeing and disagreeing, knowing and not knowing, never static. And yet into such a maelstrom the social worker is called to act. We know that in that moment, there is some error in anything we do.

Sometimes you will build bridges over troubled waters. Sometimes you will pour gasoline on smoldering embers. You will do so secure in the knowledge that you have incomplete knowledge. You are the perfect master of imperfection. This is the burden of the middleweight. It is the heavy clear vision of just how unclear things can be. It is why some people hate social workers, and why we are so needed in the world.

How will you carry it?

If you are wise, this way of knowing will make you humble. You will nourish yourself with the medicine of forgiveness, and share it generously with all the others you meet. You will embrace the uncertainty of your human interactions. You will seek strengths in the weakest of situations. You will learn the humor that can be taught by flowers. You will understand why it might be a good thing that a man has sex with cheese.

You are armed with the vision that the world is always incomplete, no matter what lens one looks through. You can never perfect this world. But in joining with others with your compassion and care, you have the responsibility now, with us, your colleagues, to try.

Letting Go

There was a wide treeless hill that rose up in that corner of far northwest Baltimore, somewhere below an apartment complex, and above the woods surrounding the old Seton Hospital, a Catholic asylum.

I must be nine years old, as I've been allowed to cross Rogers Avenue, my previous northernmost boundary, and set up my efforts at the base of this sweeping incline. The early spring sky is cold and steel-gray. Low clouds swim by like a swiftly moving blanket. It is March, and she is blowing in like a lion.

The day before, a Sunday, I had squirreled together enough money to go to Zerwitz's drugstore and buy a simple cross-stick kite kit, and a ball of string. I spent the afternoon fixing the paper structure, tightening the bow lines and guidelines, and finding the proper scraps of old sheets in the garage to make a tail. I'd built these things a number of times before, and they always turned into dismal failures after one or two attempts to put them aloft. The stick broke or the paper tore, or after a thrilling brief rip into the sky, they came crashing down to earth to bust themselves into crumpled trash. I was determined to fly one. I had seen bigger boys do it. I would have gone out that Sunday afternoon, but storms moved in and made kite flying impossible.

All day in school on Monday, I watched the rain turn into a blustery, cold, gray, day. The rain stopped, and at the end of the day, I ran home to try my luck against the hill and the wind.

None of my friends are about, and I find myself alone in that field. The air is persistent and pushes against my jacket and makes my jeans flutter about my ankles. Slowly I back myself into the wind and let the kite catch the breeze in my wake. It shudders, but does not outrageously dip and swing and crash as others have done before. It stands in the wind, at first just a few feet above and before me, clearly flying. I pull in a bit, a brief tug, and it swings higher. I release a yard of string and tug again.

Again it rose higher and farther. I repeated this over and over for what seemed like an hour. I was chilled to the bone as there had been tiny squalls of stinging rain. I could not move. I came to the end of the ball, and the line remained only in my grasp, fixed. Taut against my cold hands, the string pulled out and up into invisibility in the direction of what was now my small success, this very small kite, high and far away, black in the cold gray clouds.

I know by the developing dark and headlights of passing cars that I will soon be late to supper. I am aware of a sad little loneliness that mixes with my otherwise proud and happy heart. No one but I can stand and see this wonder of this flying small thing, dark in the darkening sky. I will never forget this moment, even as I do not understand it. I look up, then down, and then up again.

It hurts, as my fingers are stiff. I open my hand and am released.

A Silver Dollar Thank You—A Coda

Can you tell me, Socrates, whether virtue is acquired by teaching or practice, or if by neither teaching nor practice, then whether it comes to man by nature, or in some other way?

Meno, in Aristotle's *Ethics*[8]

Now comes the time when there are celebrations of accomplishment. Students become graduates. Degrees are given upon diploma. License is certified. It is a time when one status ends and another begins. It is upon such a time that I think it best to consider acts of accomplishment and acts of appreciation of how the personal derives from the efforts of the social.

Many years ago, I worked my way through undergraduate school as an orderly at a Catholic hospital down the street from where I went to college. I usually worked evening or night shifts, and was one of the few people in the hospital who might meet a patient at the ambulance, coming into the hospital at the emergency room door, and be the same person who wheeled out their body to the undertaker waiting with his hearse on the loading dock at the back of the morgue.

It was not uncommon to be paged in the night to transfer a body from the morgue to an undertaker. I would walk through the quiet sleeping hallways, up a few flights, and toward the back of the hospital. In the transit, the environment would transform from the patient floors of tile and stainless steel and isopropyl alcohol, to the wooden and golden space of administrative wings, scented with wax, under the gaze of a statue of a bleeding Mary, to the sullen concrete and cinder block of the "pathology lab" and the loading dock, the air filled with formalin.

Whoever came from the funeral home would meet me at the dock with a collapsible wheel cot and show me a form with a name upon it. They would follow me into a refrigerated space where the dead reposed upon cold metal litters, and I would search out the appropriate toe tag. In silence or with a simple "one, two, three," we would shift the deceased from the morgue litter to the transport cot. I would lock the lab door and escort the undertaker to the loading dock. I would open the door of the hearse, and with a clatter and a bang, he would trundle the cot into the vehicle. Upon slamming the door, invariably, there would be a handshake that included a silver dollar.

I don't exactly remember the first dollar I ever received, but I do remember being entirely surprised, and somewhat speechless. I had not expected to be tipped for bringing out the dead. When I asked older, experienced orderlies about this coined handshake, they nodded knowingly and responded in similar ways. "It's the Deaner's Due," said one, using an old German word for a laboratory custodian—a custom that all the funeral homes that visited the hospital respected. "Except the State Medical Examiner," said another. "You won't get the time of day from that shmoe."

I remember being made strangely uncomfortable by the passing of this silver and one night raised my hand to refuse. "I don't take tips for doing my job," I quietly stated. The undertaker smiled and lowered my hand, impressing the coin. "It's not a tip," he said, "It's a thank you. The silver makes it shine longer."

The posture of thanking can come from many directions, and there is a shift in the weight depending upon where one approaches. Many westerners come from a place of gratitude, which can largely be thought of as an emotional experience—a feeling of appreciation toward another who has extended some aid or assistance. This feeling can be warm, as one feels a solitary burden lifted with the help of another's hand. The dark side of emotional posture is the other side of gratitude's coin—a sense of indebtedness, which for some turns a burden's lift into just another burden. Sometimes, that's the challenge of emotion—its subjectiveness of personal experience.

In some eastern perspectives, one finds the Pali word *Katannuta*. A compound idea that is more cognitive than emotional. Kata being a thing that has been done to some benefit of one, Annuta being a recognition of that benefit. Implicit in the Buddhist perspective, therefore, is a simple acknowledgment that help is given and taken in this world of suffering. It is a thing in itself that passes between human beings.

In the traditions of our uniformed sea services, the Navy, Marines, and the Coast Guard, a newly commissioned ensign or lieutenant will, upon receiving the first salute, pass a silver dollar to the person who first acknowledges the shiny new bar of their rank. The tradition is furthered by the recipients pocketing the coins. Those who wish to long remember this thank you place the coin in the pocket of the right hand.

It is, I believe, a proper thing that we should say thank you. More than a personal feeling of gratitude, that act of thanksgiving recognizes that intrinsic social bond responsible for every act of accomplishment. In every learning there is both—teacher and student, master and apprentice—and it is both who engage the heavy lifting, and both who recognize its worth. It is fitting that we look eye-to-eye and recognize the mutual dependence and the collective reward. The world would be a much better place if we just thanked each other more. In the passing of thanks, we become larger than just a simple self. More worn by life, we take on a bit of shine.

A simple e-mail one afternoon came from a new junior professor at a faraway university. It was a thank you note. In it, my correspondent indicated that she had been a student of mine in one of the first years I taught in a BSW program. Now, more than a decade later, with a newly minted Ph.D., she, too, was a teacher and had come across a chapter I had written in a book she was using for her class. The piece apparently had moved her to write. She praised me for "being real and having a passion for social work."

I responded with a kind "thank you" for her gratitude, and best wishes for her future efforts teaching our profession. I did not tell her that nowhere in my mind's eye could I find a memory of her face.

It doesn't matter that I cannot find her picture. My eyes are blinded by the light. For like those of us who celebrate this day the accomplishments of becoming new social workers, I will find her face wherever I go in the world. Here in my right pocket is a bright shiny dollar, and I must pass it on.

"I want to thank you, thank you..."
Kind and Generous, Natalie Merchant[9]

Beginnings, Middles, and EndNotes

Beginnings

[1]William Schwartz was a social worker in the 1950s who went on to become a social work educator at a number of universities. He co-wrote a very influential book on group work, *The Practice of Group-work*, in 1971 with Sarapio Zalba. Although he wrote relatively little, he influenced a great many social workers who have written much about his "interactionist" perspective.

[2]Johann Wolfgang von Goethe (1749–1832) was an artist, scientist, lawyer, and politician who had a great effect on many other famous thinkers of the nineteenth century. He wrote novels, plays, poetry, essays, criticism, and scientific works that provoked many of the ideas leading to modern thought.

[3]Flow State: Mihaly Csikszentmihalyi became interested in artists who would get lost in their work. Artists (and athletes and social workers) can get so immersed in their work that they lose all track of time. See Csikszentmihalyi, Mihaly (1998). *Finding Flow: The Psychology of Engagement With Everyday Life.* New York: Basic Books.

[4]The Interstate Highway system, which began in 1956, probably has played a major role in the development of "suburban life," issues of sustainability, quality of life in urban America, and the inconsistent availability of public transportation.

[5]A Foley catheter is a flexible tube that is passed through the urethra and into the bladder to drain urine from the body. Inserting one is a somewhat uncomfortable experience for the patient.

[6]Freud, Anna. (1937). *The Ego and the Mechanisms of Defense,* London: Hogarth Press and Institute of Psycho-Analysis. (Revised edition: 1966).

[7]An ostomy pouching system (commonly called a bag) is a medical prosthetic that provides a mechanism for collecting biological waste from a surgically diverted organ system such as the colon.

[8]Shulman, Lawrence. (2009). *The Skills of Helping Individuals, Families, Groups, and Communities.* Belmont, CA: Brooks-Cole. Shulman is a social work writer who has been very influenced by William Schwartz.

[9]Pearce, Joseph Chilton. (1973). *The crack in the cosmic egg: challenging constructs of mind and reality.* New York: Pocket Books.

[10]Joseph Wolpe (1915-1997) was one of the most influential figures in "behavior therapy." Wolpe was famous for treatment of phobia with "Systematic Desensitization," in which a patient is exposed to the anxiety producing stimulus at a low level, and perhaps taught a relaxation technique as well. There is a stepwise exposure to stronger aspects of the stimulus until the patient no longer feels any anxiety toward the stimulus.

[11]Erving Goffman (1922–1982) was an influential sociologist who wrote on such ideas as "role" theory, stigma, labeling, and the effect of "institutions" on behavior. He wrote several books, all of them quite readable. I encourage you to read him.

[12]Jean Henri Dunant, (1828–1910), also known as Henry Dunant, was a Swiss businessman, social activist, and father of the Red Cross movement. In 1859, he witnessed the terrible Battle of Solferino in Italy. He wrote a book about the battle, *A Memory of Solferino,* which inspired the birth of the International Committee of the Red Cross and the first Geneva Convention. In 1901, he was a co-recipient of the first Nobel Peace Prize.

[13]Terkel, Studs. (1974). *Working: People Talk About What They Do All Day and How They Feel About What They Do.* New York: Pantheon Books.

[14]Refers to the September 11, 2001, al-Qaeda terrorist attack in which airplanes were flown into the World Trade Center in New York City and the Pentagon in Washington, D.C.

Middles

[1]Ruth E. Smalley was a social worker, as well as Professor and Dean of the School of Social Work at the University of Pennsylvania. Along with her colleagues at "the Penn School," Jessie Taft and Virginia Robinson, all influenced by psychoanalyst Otto Rank, she was a proponent of what became known as the "Functional" model of social work practice in the 1940s and 50s. "Functional" theory placed emphasis on putting a "function" into the middle of a social work relationship that both the client and worker could use to help establish clarity about what needed to occur in the helping process.

[2]A short reference for someone suffering from Parkinson's disease, a degenerative disorder of the central nervous system that has no clear etiology. I should never have used this term for another human being suffering from this terrible and slowly wasting condition.

[3]Maugham, W. Somerset. (2008). *The Razor's Edge,* New York: Random House.

[4]On November 6, 2001, then President Bush made this statement concerning the "War on Terror." I struggled with his attempt to simplify such a complex situation.

[5]NASW Code of Ethics. Dignity and worth of the person. Important value and responsibility worth long and continuous consideration.

[6]The United States Public Health Service has an all-officer "Commissioned Corps" of uniformed health care personnel, including many social workers, who perform many important functions in military environments, disasters, U.S. prisons, and the Indian Health Service.

[7]P-I-E is short for "Person-in-Environment," sometimes also known as "Person-in Situation," perhaps the central perspective in the "social work way of knowing"...but then, you knew that, didn't you?

The Dialogues of Hanna

[1]Lao-Tzu. (1992). *The Tao Te Ching.* New York: Harper Collins. An ancient Chinese Taoist text. Well worth the read and consideration.

[2]Sun-Tzu. (1963). *The Art of War,* translated and annotated by Samuel B. Griffith. London: Oxford University Press. An Ancient Chinese military text. Also well worth the read and consideration.

[3]A paraphrase from *Henry The Sixth, Part 2 Act 4, scene 2, 71–78,* by William Shakespeare. Many of Shakespeare's plays operate with language and plot that work at many levels at once. Reading Shakespeare gives one, I believe, an appreciation for the multiple meanings of words and helps develop a depth of critical mind.

[4]Alinsky, Saul. (1971). *Rules for Radicals,* New York: Vintage Books. Saul D. Alinsky (1909–1972) was an American community organizer and writer. He is considered to be an influential figure in the theory and practice of community organizing.

[5]Patrick O'Brian (1914–2000) was an author best known for his "Aubrey–Maturin" series of novels of the Napoleonic Wars. There are some 20 novels about life in the Royal Navy during the 19th century. He uses rich language, and I've read several of them as a way of escapist recreation.

[6]SAMHSA is the Substance Abuse & Mental Health Service Administration, a division of the U.S. Department of Health & Human Services.

[7]Friedrich Wilhelm Nietzsche (1844–1900) was a German philosopher, poet, composer, and cultural critic. He wrote critical texts on religion, morality, culture, philosophy, and science. He was influenced by the philosopher, Arthur Schopenhauer, and his popular works include *Beyond Good and Evil, On Truth and Lies in a Nonmoral Sense,* and *Thus Spoke Zarathustra.*

[8]Ayn Rand (1905-1982) was a Russian-American novelist and economic philosopher. She is known for two best-selling novels, *The Fountainhead* and *Atlas Shrugged,* which provide illustration of a philosophical system she called "Objectivism." Much of Rand's work celebrates radical individualism and free-market thinking. Social workers should read her work and then come to their own decisions as to how to argue with her perspectives.

[9]Whitman, Walt. (1959). *Leaves of Grass.* New York: Viking Press. A classic collection of poetry by one of America's first modern poets.

[10]Leonard Cohen (1934) is a singer-songwriter, musician, poet, and novelist.

[11]Otto Rank (1884–1939) was an Austrian psychoanalyst, writer, and teacher. He was one of Sigmund Freud's closest colleagues for 20 years, but the two had a falling out when Rank posited a developmental theory of psychoanalysis opposing Freud's more deterministic theory. He greatly influenced "The Functional School" of social work that arose out of the University of Pennsylvania in the late 1930s. Many modern humanistic psychotherapists and writers have acknowledged that Rank played a significant role in their thinking.

[12]That really is the question, isn't it?

Ends

[1]Inger Stevens was a television and motion picture actress who suffered from life-long depression and died of an overdose in the 1970s.

[2]*The Way We Were.* (1973). An American romantic drama film, starring Barbra Streisand and Robert Redford, directed by Sydney Pollack.

[3]The United States Department of Veterans Affairs (VA) is a government-run military veteran benefit system with Cabinet-level status.

It is the United States government's second largest department, after the United States Department of Defense, and is one of the country's largest employers of clinical social workers.

[4]The term "looking glass self" was first used by Charles Horton Cooley in *Human Nature and the Social Order* (1902). A social psychological concept, the term refers to people shaping their self-concepts based on their understanding of how others perceive them.

[5]Reverse Trendelenburg position is a way of positioning a patient in a hospital bed so the patient is lying flat on his/her back, with the head higher than the feet by about 15-30 degrees.

[6]Decathexis is a psychoanalytical term that describes the withdrawal of cathexis from an idea or object. Cathexis is defined as the process of investment of mental or emotional energy in a person, object, or idea. If you read Elisabeth Kübler-Ross' *On Death and Dying* (1969) very carefully, you will see this is the real last stage of grief.

[7]Thomas Aquinas (1225–1274), also known as Saint Thomas of Aquin, was an Italian Dominican priest, and an immensely influential philosopher and theologian. His most famous work is the *Summa Theologica*.

[8]Bartlett, Robert C., & Collins, Susan D. (eds.). (2012). *Aristotle's Nicomachean Ethics*. Chicago: University of Chicago Press.

[9]Merchant, Natalie. (1998). *Kind and Generous*. On Ophelia. New York: Elektra Records (Warner Music Group).

About the Author

Ogden W. Rogers, Ph.D., LCSW, ACSW, is Professor and Chair of the Department of Social Work at The University of Wisconsin-River Falls. He has been a clinician, consultant, educator, and storyteller. Dr. Rogers began his social work career in community and adult psychiatry in both inpatient and outpatient settings. He's worked in emergency and critical-care medicine, disaster mental health, and mental health program delivery and evaluation in both public and private auspices. In more recent years, he's been actively involved with the American Red Cross International Services Division concerning human rights in armed conflict.

When asked about how he got involved with making a career in social work, he smiled and said, "That reminds me of a story...."

Other Social Work Titles Published by White Hat Communications

Days in the Lives of Social Workers
More Days in the Lives of Social Workers
Days in the Lives of Gerontological Social Workers
Riding the Mutual Aid Bus and Other Adventures in Group Work
Is It Ethical?
The Field Placement Survival Guide
The Social Work Graduate School Applicant's Handbook
The New Social Worker Magazine

Visit us online at:

The New Social Worker Online
http://www.socialworker.com

SocialWorkJobBank
http://www.socialworkjobbank.com

White Hat Communications Store
http://shop.whitehatcommunications.com

Beginnings, Middles, & Ends (web site for this book)
http://www.beginningsmiddlesandends.com

Network with us:

http://www.facebook.com/newsocialworker
http://www.facebook.com/socialworkjobbank
http://www.facebook.com/daysinthelivesofsocialworkers
http://www.facebook.com/whitehatcommunications
http://www.twitter.com/newsocialworker
http://www.linkedin.com/groups?gid=3041069
https://plus.google.com/101612885418842828982/posts